A Voice For Kathy

"Silent Threads: Weaving Truth, Spreading Light"

By

Jean-Davis Thomson

Dedication

This book is dedicated to my beloved daughter Kathy, whose life ended far too soon. Your vivacious spirit could light up any room. Your empathy and kindness lifted up all who knew you. I miss your infectious laugh and unwavering love every moment of every day.

I also dedicate this to all daughters who see traces of themselves in Kathy's story. May you find the courage to walk your own path, unburden your heart when it grows too heavy, and never doubt your intrinsic worth. As a mother, I wish I could gather you under my wings and shelter you from all harm. But know you already possess the strength within to weather any storm.

To all mothers, may we never take for granted the sacred privilege of guiding our children. Though we cannot shield them from life's pain, our love remains their most powerful armor. Keep your heart open, judgement withheld, wisdom ready to impart when sought. Our work is never finished.

This is in loving memory of my son John, whose unconditional love lifts me still. You are ever in my thoughts, my purpose and inspiration. I could not be more proud of the life you built upon the foundations we laid together. You are my rock, my refuge. My love for you stretches beyond earthly bounds.

This book became my path to healing after losing two children in one year. I walk this road for all mothers who know the anguish of outliving a child. May you find comfort knowing their light can never be extinguished. It shines on in every cherished memory and ripples outward in the hearts they've touched. We carry their legacies forward. From the depths of pain, may we harvest wisdom, courage and above all, kindness, knowing they are never far from our side. For life and death, joy and sorrow, we walk this winding path together. We are never alone.

Acknowledgements of Thanks

So many to thank throughout this journey of life and most recently, writing *A Voice For Kathy*. Thanks especially to my writer/publisher who encouraged me to tell Kathy's story and instilled in me the courage, strength and confidence to share it in a book to make Kathy's voice heard through me.

I'm forever thankful for all the people who have touched my life, and the lives of my children, in any way throughout my lifetime. Friends and family have always surrounded me through good and bad times. Thank you for your unwavering love and support. I am looking forward to whatever the future holds. My siblings and their families have always been my best friends and offered a secure haven for a sometimes lost and lonely soul.

God Bless my prayer warrior, Gloria, whose link to God was my inspiration and who has deepened my faith beyond belief as John and Kathy completed their journey in this world. I'm grateful for every prayer and kind gesture from every person who took the time to think about us. I thank Father Kelly for his bedside goodbye to John as the angels carried him home after a long and relentless battle for life.

I thank my amazing, beloved daughter, Laurie, and her incredible husband, Tom, for their unconditional love, caring and for blessing me with five of the most amazing grandchildren and their families... each one a very special and irreplaceable gift from God. John's son, daughters and grandsons, live on as a part of him and offer healing for that empty space in my heart.

I am grateful to my Mother and Father, deceased for many

years, for giving me and my siblings a steadfast foundation in the Christian Faith and setting the example of love, respect and integrity... qualities that pave the pathway to a rewarding life.

I have cried an ocean of tears. However, knowing Kathy's story might make a difference in someone else's life, fills my heart with gratitude and helps contribute to the difficult healing process. I can't bring Kathy and John back, but I can recognize that their lives had a profound and worthwhile purpose and I find enormous consolation in those thoughts. Their lives were an overwhelming and priceless blessing to me and to others... they will continue to live in my heart forever.

Love,

Jean

Table of Contents

Foreword

A Journey of Resilience and Hope

I have always been a profoundly private person, guarding the sanctity of my life with a tenacious resolve. My world, from its very inception, revolved exclusively around the well-being of my children. The past, a Pandora's box of memories, remained firmly locked away, shrouded in silence. However, now, the time has come to unseal the hidden chapters and unveil the stories that have remained veiled for so long.

The journey I embarked upon in my early thirties was a tempestuous one, a maelstrom that threatened to engulf the serene existence my children and I had carefully constructed. The mantle of responsibility for their welfare weighed heavily on my shoulders as I grappled with the ruins of my marriage. Despite my most earnest efforts to salvage it, I couldn't stave off the inevitable collapse. The anguish of feeling I had failed my children, who were innocent bystanders to the sadness and emotional turmoil, was an all-encompassing torrent.

The most poignant chapter of this saga was the departure of my soon-to-be ex-husband. With a heart as frigid as the coldest winter, he left us, forsaking not only our family but also his responsibilities, abandoning a chaos that I, alone, had to navigate. It felt like a storm of mayhem, and I had no choice but to cleanse the wreckage and provide for my family. The only consolation was that he could not elude the repercussions of his actions, regardless of how far he journeyed.

A handful of loyal friends stood steadfastly by my side, offering unwavering support during those trying times. Yet, my own insecurities often acted as a wall, keeping others at an arm's length. I found myself adrift in an ocean of uncertainty, feeling powerless and bereft of control over the course of my life. The burden was mine to bear, and I had to discover a path to keep my family intact.

As I reflect on these memories now, the notion of committing my story to the written word is something I never thought I could undertake, nor did I ever harbor the desire to do so. There are some moments from the past that are far easier to obliterate, to inter them in a remote corner of memory rather than confront their stark realities. However, I came to realize that I could not alter the past. My best recourse was to embrace a fresh beginning and to give my utmost to construct a new life, one that bore the promise of fulfillment.

Amid the turmoil of this period, I clung steadfastly to my unwavering positivity and my unyielding work ethic. These qualities eventually led me to secure a position as a secretary to an executive banker. In this new arena, I found not only the means to provide for my family but also a sense of purpose and self-reliance.

A decade later, life took an unexpected turn when I crossed paths with my second husband, Clay Davis. Clay, a retired military veteran and the proprietor of three thriving travel agencies, became a beacon of hope in my life. He not only embraced my children, adopting my son and extending his arms to my daughters, but he also played a pivotal role in helping me rebuild my self-esteem, granting me the freedom to dream beyond the constraints of my past. With his mentorship and unwavering support, I transitioned into a career in the travel industry, embarking on a journey that bore the promise of a brighter future.

Yet, as life often demonstrates, joy was tinged with sorrow. Our marriage, despite its warmth and promise, was curtailed by the cruel hand of fate, as cancer claimed Clay's life. The news of his passing was a devastating shock to all of us, a jarring reminder of the fragility of life. My son lost the father he held in deep affection, and I lost the husband I cherished, setting us on a course to navigate yet another profound shift in the tapestry of our lives.

Clay's passing and John's diagnosis with juvenile diabetes delivered a double blow to our family. I lived in perpetual fear of losing my son, but we somehow navigated the challenges and made the necessary adjustments. The support we received from our loved ones and friends served as our guiding light through those turbulent times. A few years later, I decided to make a significant move, taking John with me to Florida. He was just 15 years old when Kathy and Laurie decided to tie the knot.

The decision to relocate to Florida was driven by the belief that its climate would be more suitable for John's diabetic condition, not to mention the allure of year-round sunshine and fresh air. It was an exciting change, one that promised new beginnings and opportunities.

In Florida, I opened a travel agency and immersed myself in the local community, participating in various organizations and fundraising efforts. The days were long, filled with hard work, and I made regular visits to Kathy and Laurie. John was juggling college and working at the agency, and I couldn't have been prouder of his determination and resilience.

As time went by, I became acquainted with Bob, a presence in my life since my move to Florida. Bob was married at the time, and I had the privilege of sharing many dinners at their home.

Bob had a passion for cooking. Tragically, his wife succumbed to cancer, and it was after this loss that Bob and I began dating.

A year later, we took the plunge and got married. Together, we built a beautiful house in Niceville and enjoyed 22 wonderful years, filled with travel, golf, and the warmth of cherished friendships. However, life had its own plan, and Bob passed away on April 4, 2015, leaving behind a treasure trove of memories.

Through all the twists and turns, my wisdom and personal growth continued to expand. Life had thrown an assortment of challenges my way, but it had also opened doors to unexpected opportunities. With every experience, I felt myself evolving and maturing, a process that added depth to the chapters of my life. I couldn't help but believe that this remarkable journey had more in store for me.

My current challenge, a monumental one, is to seek justice for my daughter's untimely death. I grapple with questions that have remained unanswered for far too long. The justice system failed her, as did her husband. Yet, I found myself at a crossroads, unsure of where to turn for the answers and the support required to secure justice for Kathy. While my faith in God's justice system remained steadfast, the human justice system was an enigma. Money often took precedence over justice, but I remained hopeful, knowing that there were individuals who did the right thing.

In the meantime, I am determined to make Kathy's voice heard. My mission in sharing Kathy's story is to illuminate a path for others, one that might help them avoid the tears and pain that my family endured. Dealing with the loss of a child is heart-wrenching, but when it's compounded by questionable circumstances, the pain becomes unbearable. My hope is that, in telling Kathy's story, we can start the healing process, finding solace in the belief that Kathy's life was a gift to others.

I stand at this crossroads, I can't help but wonder what other chapters await in the story of my life. The journey has been a testament to strength, resilience, and unwavering hope, and I believe it's far from over. Life has a way of surprising us, and I'm ready to embrace whatever comes next.

Heartstrings and Hardships

It was a bright morning of 2022 when I arrived in the charming coastal town of Lewes, Delaware. As I stepped out of the car and took in the quaint shops lining the main street, I could feel the excitement bubbling up inside me. This was the start of a new chapter in my life.

After spending most of my adult years in the sunny climes of Florida, I was embarking on a fresh adventure up north to be closer to my daughter Laurie, her husband Tom, and their wonderful family. Laurie and her family had moved to Lewes a few years back and I was eager to join them in this picturesque town by the sea.

The morning sun glinted off the water as I strolled down to the marina. Breathing in the salty air, I felt a sense of hope and possibility. Being near Laurie and Tom again would be like finding a warm, welcoming harbor after being tossed about in choppy waters for far too long.

Life had thrown me more than my share of storms over the past 5 decades. I was thrust into the role of being a single parent to three wonderful children after their father abruptly abandoned us. I still vividly remember the day he left. The kids had just started another semester of the school year. Kathleen had just turned 12, Laura was 11, and little John had only recently celebrated his fourth birthday. I didn't know where to begin as their father left town with no forwarding address and he never looked back. He didn't even show up for the divorce proceedings.

I broke the news to the kids as gently as I could. There were many tears and unanswerable questions. "Why did daddy leave?" little John kept asking. But I had no good reply. The truth was I simply didn't know.

Over the next several months, I struggled to make sense of it all myself. My husband's disappearance left me reeling both financially and emotionally. I was now the sole provider for three young children. We had to move to a smaller house in a less expensive neighborhood. I took whatever office jobs I could find while trying to balance caring for the kids.

The divorce proceedings themselves were almost anti-climactic. With my husband opting to sever all ties, it was just a legal formality finalizing what he had made abundantly clear through his absence. But the lack of closure weighed on all of us. For the kids, the pain of abandonment loomed large. They missed their father desperately despite his disappearance from their lives. I did my best to fill both parental roles but it was far from easy.

Still, we persevered. As the kids adjusted to new schools and a new life with just mom, I worked tirelessly to keep us afloat. Kathleen and Laura grew into wonderful young women. And little John slowly left his boyhood behind and entered adolescence, taking up water skiing, camping and enjoying normal fun and activities with friends of his age. One of his favorite times was whenever he could spend time with his sisters.

By 1981, over a decade had passed since that tragic incident in our lives. The kids were now young adults making their way in the world. Kathy and Laurie were young adults pursuing college and John was a young boy entering his teens.

And then on March 7, 1981, fate surprised me with a blessing I never could have expected. I remarried, to a kind and generous man named Clay. He was a retired air force pilot and a complete gentleman. With his loving support, I felt a sense of renewal unlike anything I had experienced since my carefree youth.

Clay's presence quickly became a stabilizing force for all of us. He took a special interest in John, acting as the caring father figure he had missed for so many years. Clay recounted riveting stories from his flying days, captivating John's imagination. He was the mentor and role model my son had long needed.

Within a year, Clay officially adopted John, cementing their bond. Kathleen and Laura adored their new stepfather as well. I will never forget the joy I felt seeing my family whole again on the day that adoption was finalized, knowing we had weathered the storm.

I had found my way to calmer waters. My newly expanded family was now my safe harbor and I couldn't wait to make memories together. The past was behind me. My gaze was set on the bright horizon ahead. This next chapter would surely be filled with laughter, joy and the simple pleasures of spending time with loved ones. It was a new beginning forged from the ashes of what came before. As I held hands with Clay and found relief in his warm hugs, I was ready to start the next chapter of my life.

The Shadows of Grief

Tragedy, an uninvited guest, reared its somber head once again. A mere 14 months after the union that brought renewed hope, my beloved husband Clay was dealt a devastating blow - a diagnosis of brain cancer. The cosmic clock ticked relentlessly, and on August 25, 1982, God beckoned him home, leaving behind an irreplaceable void in our lives.

As if fated by cruel circumstance, the universe unfolded an additional layer of adversity. In the very week that witnessed Clay's departure, our son John received a life-altering diagnosis of Juvenile Diabetes. Fate, it seemed, had conspired to test our resilience to the fullest. The poignant irony manifested as both father and son found themselves ensconced in the sterile confines of the hospital simultaneously. The medical staff, perhaps unwittingly, placed John in a room a mere door away from his ailing father, creating a heart-wrenching proximity that underscored the fragility of life.

The cruel synchronicity reached its zenith when Clay's funeral unfolded, and John, having a hospital pass, briefly escaped the confines of medical care to bid a tearful farewell to his departed father. The hospital pass, a bittersweet ticket to grieve, required John's prompt return to the hospital as diligent doctors sought to regulate his newfound companion, Juvenile Diabetes. Each moment of solace was juxtaposed with the pressing need for medical oversight, a delicate dance between mourning and managing a chronic condition.

Adaptation became our newfound mantra, and the corridors of the hospital transformed into a classroom where we learned the intricacies of navigating life with diabetes. For me, the role of caregiver took on an added dimension, a responsibility that demanded both emotional fortitude and unwavering commitment. John, resilient in the face of adversity, forged ahead with life, while I, the ever-watchful guardian, remained tethered to the pendulum of concern.

The narrative took an unexpected turn on June 25, 1993, when I embraced a new chapter of companionship with Bob. Over the course of 22 joy-laden years, we weathered life's storms together before he, too, succumbed on April 4, 2015. Bob became more than a life partner; he was the anchor that steadied me when the tempest of John's health threatened to overwhelm. The intricacies of caregiving, a role I had grown accustomed to, found a renewed companion in Bob, and our shared journey became a testament to the strength found in unity.

Reflecting on the years with John and Bob, I am enveloped in a profound sense of gratitude for the blessings bestowed upon me. Good health, a resilient spirit, and the capacity to navigate the intricate dance of caregiving defined my journey. In the tapestry of life, I wouldn't unravel a single thread, for each moment, however laden with challenges, contributed to the rich mosaic of my existence.

The shadows of grief cast their long, harrowing tendrils over my life as I grappled with the profound loss of my youngest child, John. In January of 2022, at the age of 51, he succumbed to the relentless challenges posed by Juvenile Diabetes, a battle he had valiantly fought since the tender age of 12. Throughout the years, John had confronted numerous episodes of severe health crises, defying the specter of death with a resilience that bordered on the miraculous.

Me and John — A Year Before He Died

His indomitable spirit faced its ultimate test in September of 2014 when a debilitating stroke struck, altering the trajectory of his life irreversibly. Undeterred, John embarked on the arduous journey of recovery, displaying a bravery that became emblematic of his character. Despite the odds, he had weathered previous life-threatening moments, but this time, the stroke left an indelible mark. The once vibrant soul now found himself confined to a wheelchair, stripped of the ability to care for himself or embrace the independence he had once known.

John carved out a peaceful existence surrounded by nature's beauty in the Pocono Mountains. The tranquility brought him comfort and glimpses of heaven. As I raced between caring for my ailing husband and supporting John's rehabilitation needs, my resilience was tested to the brink.

The years unfolded in a relentless procession of anguish, each moment etched with the silent screams of a mother watching her child endure unimaginable pain. The emotional toll, at times, threatened to overwhelm, a torrent of grief that no words could adequately articulate. The nightmare of losing a child, regardless of their age, transcended the boundaries of comprehension, creating a bond with a grief-stricken club no parent willingly joins.

After John's funeral, I briefly reunited with my daughter Kathy in February. Her physical and emotional pain had kept her from attending the services. Embracing her delicate frame, I never imagined it would be our last tender moment together after kissing her goodbye at the end of our visit.

From: <JTDevis228@aol.com>

To: <mixmatch1@cox.net>

Sent: Sunday, June 16, 2002 5:51 AM

Subject: **Happy Father's Day**

Bob:

I know you got our card, but I wanted to send you a special email for this special occasion. The email you sent last night touched both Anna and myself very deeply, and we are proud that you are part of our family. It comes with great pride when I speak of you to Anna's family and tell them that you are my step-dad. I have three fathers, but now you are the only one that I can really speak to. My first father as you know, abandoned us, so he never got the privilege of being a father. The second one, although only in my life for a short time, took the role of being my father and tried to pass along as much of his wisdom to me as possible, but unfortunately I lost him. Now, I have you to consider as my father, my mentor, my friend. Even though I was grown and moved out of the house, I never stopped learning from you. You have taught me what honor is, and what it is like to be an individual. You have taught me how to be a man, to stick up for what is right, and to treat those around me with respect. You have played just as much a part in my life as Clay did. For all of that, and for the things that I have not mentioned, I am forever thankful, not only to have you as a father, but just to have you in my life. One thing I never mentioned to you, is that, whenever I was in the wrong, even though I didn't show it, I always felt bad that I had let you down in some way. A father is always a hero to his kids, and you have been a hero to me several times. I love you as my father and always will. So, Happy Father's Day Bob, you deserve it, not just for today, but every day.

Love,

John and Anna

A note my son John wrote to my husband Bob for Father's Day

Tragedy Strikes Again

The cruel hand of fate was not done tormenting my family. Just 8 short months after we bid farewell to my son John, tragedy struck again. This time it claimed my eldest daughter, Kathy.

Losing two of my children in less than a year felt unfathomable. The pain cut so much deeper because the circumstances around Kathy's death were questionable. As a grieving mother, I was thrust into a bewildering search for answers and understanding. But Kathy's husband Ron remained tight-lipped, almost silent in the face of my pleas. His refusal to provide any details compounded my anguish exponentially.

In my desperation, I asked Ron again and again, "what happened in her final hours?" But his response never wavered..."I don't know." He claimed ignorance about the entire situation. But his evasive demeanor betrayed a resentment simmering just below the surface.

From what little information I could gather, Kathy was in and out of consciousness for over 24 agonizing hours before Ron finally called 911. He left her lying helpless on the bare floor the entire time. His apparent indifference to her deteriorating condition perplexed and haunted me. What kind of husband shows such callous disregard for his wife's health? His neglectful actions raised so many painful questions. But Ron continued to guard the truth behind a wall of stubborn silence.

My daughter Laurie, her loyal husband Tom, and I embarked on the heartbreaking journey to attend Kathy's funeral in Miami. The fog of shock and disbelief clung to us like a suffocating shroud. Attending my child's funeral so soon after burying my son felt like some nightmarish dream. I moved through those mournful days in a daze, numb to the reality that my vibrant, beautiful Kathy was truly gone.

The world marched on around me. But inwardly, I struggled to reconcile my new reality. The empty space left by Kathy's absence reverberated with our unfinished conversations and wasted moments we could never get back. Her premature death carved a gaping void where cherished memories now lived. I knew I would need to draw on these memories for strength to endure the lonely years ahead without her.

I still replay that final conversation, when Kathy promised she would see a doctor about concerning symptoms that mirrored John's diabetic issues. That vow echoed hauntingly after she was gone. Perhaps if I had recognized the gravity in her words, I could have saved her. But in my distressed state, I missed the signs.

Then in September, a call from Laurie shattered my world yet again. She relayed the news from Kathy's husband Ron - Kathy was in intensive care clinging to life. I was devastated and flooded with questions. Just days prior, Kathy and I had discussed her dream of retiring in Delaware near family. What had gone so wrong in just a few months?

Desperate to rush to her side, I prepared to travel to Florida immediately. But Ron pleaded for me not to come. The prognosis was too grim, he warned that she likely would not survive the night. His solemn words landed like a crushing blow to my fragile hopes.

Then mere hours later, Laurie's phone call sealed my worst fear. ***"Kathy has passed away,"*** she wept. My beautiful daughter was gone. What should have been the tranquil sunset of her life was cut short by tragedy once more.

The Ordeal

In that moment, shock became an insufficient word to encapsulate the tsunami of emotions that cascaded over me. The surreal landscape of grief unfolded, and I found myself standing on the precipice of an unfathomable loss—two children, gone within eight months of each other.

Not once did her husband extend the courtesy of a call, a lifeline of communication, during pivotal moments—Kathy's fall, the excruciating 24 hours she languished on the floor in dire need, or even during her hospitalization. The enigma of his actions perplexed me, shrouding the circumstances in a cloak of confusion.

In the immediate aftermath of Laurie's call, bearing the devastating news of Kathy's critical condition, I felt compelled to reach out to her husband. The conversation, however, unveiled a disturbing truth—he was woefully uninformed about the timeline of Kathy's ordeal. When queried about her hospital arrival, his response only deepened the mystery, as he claimed she reached the hospital overnight. Yet, the harrowing reality, extracted from independent sources and hospital records, revealed that Kathy had been in critical condition for two nights before her eventual admission, enduring an additional 24 hours alone and in distress.

The stark revelation of Kathy's protracted suffering, exacerbated by her husband's neglect to promptly seek assistance or notify her mother, haunts my nights. The vivid nightmares paint a cruel tableau of my daughter lying helpless on the floor, grappling with the harshness of inhumane treatment. It is an unthinkable scenario, a betrayal of the fundamental human instinct to lend aid to those in need. The relentless grip of diabetes claimed her life during those agonizing hours of unattended distress, extinguishing the flame of a vibrant soul with unimaginable cruelty.

In the wake of this tragic loss, the contours of my life underwent a seismic shift. Laurie and her husband, Tom, had chosen Delaware as their retirement haven, compelling me to reassess my own trajectory.

The decision to move closer to one of my daughters became imperative, and after nearly four decades in Florida, the time had come for a transformative change. Conversations with my daughters, rooted in conviction, guided my choice to relocate.

Kathy and her sister, Laurie

At the time, Laurie's plans had solidified, while Kathy's aspirations were still in the nascent stages. It was a moment of decisive action, and with the sale of my Florida home, I embarked on a journey to reside just a block away from Laurie and Tom.

The new home, nestled in proximity to family, proved to be a haven of solace, a sanctuary where I could maintain my independence while having the comfort of loved ones nearby. In this moment of transition, I felt the guiding hand of God, ushering me forward. The decision to move was not merely a geographical shift; it was a profound commitment to embrace the future, to march resolutely ahead without the shackles of the past. Gratitude welled within me for the proximity of family during these tumultuous times.

As the echoes of Kathy's passing reverberated, Laurie's call, delivered a few hours later, crystallized the irreversible reality—Kathy had departed from this world. The collective grief, shared within the confines of familial bonds, became the impetus to forge ahead, propelled by the strength derived from unity and the unwavering support of those closest to me.

Regrettably, I was not there to cradle her, to share in the solace of prayer, a reality that haunts my thoughts to this day. Had her husband extended the simple gesture of reaching out when she fell, the comforting presence of her sister and me might have been there to envelop her in a cocoon of support. If he had called and told us she fell, I know I would have screamed to call 911 at the condition she was in when I left her in February. She fell the first time either Monday or Tuesday morning. The speculative "what ifs" linger, a testament to the potential solace that might have altered the course of her fate.

The haunting specter of her solitary departure, devoid of familial warmth, resonates deeply. Her husband's absence during those critical moments, as the celestial beings carried her home, echoes with an unsettling void. It is a profound lament, a denouncement of his failure to hold her hand and provide the solace that a loved one deserves in their final moments. The visceral grief is compounded by the acknowledgment that her departure could have been a shared experience, a collective farewell that transcended the loneliness of her final breaths.

Reflecting on my interactions with her husband, I am left grappling with a disconcerting realization. Despite my explicit request for a Catholic priest to be summoned immediately, a request I believed was heeded, investigations post-funeral revealed a disconcerting truth. No such request was ever made to the hospital or the nearby Catholic Churches, as affirmed by both my independent inquiries and those conducted by the hospital ministry. The revelation stirs a tumult of emotions, from disbelief to profound disappointment, underscoring the solemnity of a missed opportunity for spiritual solace in Kathy's final moments.

However, amidst the void left by human absence, a comforting revelation emerges from the shadows. The hospital ministry divulged that a compassionate nurse in the Intensive Care Unit had independently requested a minister to offer prayers for Kathy during her final moments. The entire hospital ICU staff caring for her, assembled in a poignant display of solidarity, joining in collective prayer as Kathy transitioned from this world. The knowledge that she was surrounded by prayer, even from afar, brings a measure of solace, reinforcing the belief that, for those who hold faith dear, the divine presence is an unwavering constant.

A Year of Challenges

The year 2023 continued to unleash blow after devastating blow. Coping with the monumental loss of my son a year earlier had already tipped my world off kilter. Then the painful reality of life without my daughter Kathy threatened to pull the rug out completely. The nonstop grief took a severe toll on my health. I found myself teetering on the edge of disaster.

On April 4th, 2023, exactly eight years since my husband Bob's passing on that same tragic date, I suffered a nearly fatal heart attack. My body and spirit were pushed to the breaking point.

But by the grace of God and the love of family, I persevered through the crucible. My unshakable bond with my daughter Laurie and her loyal husband Tom became the lifeline that kept me afloat in the tempest. The hospital morphed into a battlefield where the fight for my life raged on. With each rising sun, my faith grew stronger, bolstering my will to carry on.

I'll never forget the surgeon visiting my bedside the morning after the harrowing surgery. *"You must have had an angel on each shoulder to have made it through this one,"* he remarked with awe, aware of the tremendous personal losses I had just endured.

I knew in my heart Bob and Clay were watching over me from above. They took John and Kathy's hands and said, *"Your mother needs us now."* And with that divine intervention, the steady hands of my surgeon and nursing staff brought me back from the brink.

The date of my heart attack will forever remind me that

God, not chance, charts our destiny. Even in our darkest moments, He finds ways to make His presence known, to grab our attention and show us we're not alone.

Miracles do happen – I'm living proof. I know my daughter Laurie pleaded for one as I lay unconscious in the operating room. I'm so thankful He heard her prayer and allowed me to carry on. After all, my work here isn't finished. I still have so much living left to do with my loved ones, especially in my new home in Delaware.

As I reflected on my survival, the mantra *"Jesus, I Trust In You"* reverberated through me. My faith shone like a beacon, reminding me that even when all seems lost, the Lord remains by our side. I emerged from the fire with my belief renewed and stronger than ever.

With Kathy gone, the heavy mantle of finding answers about her final days now rested solely on my shoulders. Her husband Ron passed away just two months after her, leaving me as her next of kin to pursue the truth.

I embarked on a tireless mission to unravel the mysteries surrounding her demise. I combed through every hospital record, ambulance report, and police document I could access for clues. My unwavering resolve stemmed from the burning need to make sense of it all, to honor Kathy's memory by shining a light into the shadows.

My longing for one last open and honest conversation with my daughter remained unfulfilled. The desire to unburden our hearts completely had always been hindered by her husband Ron's watchful presence. Even at lunch together, his gaze discouraged us from venturing into deeper waters.

Looking back, the signs of Kathy's inner turmoil were there, yet muted. Her gentle demeanor concealed emotional scars I can now see more clearly. Her trademark laugh often masked profound frustrations I wish she had felt safe to share.

It pains me to realize Kathy mirrored my own tendency to internalize struggles behind a convincing facade. My tumultuous first marriage had conditioned me to lock away hardship and endure in silence. Like mother, like daughter. The similarities make my heart ache over the pain she hid so adeptly.

Combing through my past, I'm reminded of how trauma shaped us both. I, too, shielded my abuser for years, allowing his behavior to fester inside unspoken. Kathy learned too well from me the dance of projecting strength on the outside while crumbling within.

When my first husband abandoned us with no explanation, I recognized that steely resilience immediately in Kathy. She tended to bury emotions as I did, relying on inner grit rather than vulnerability. Looking back, I see how profoundly our experiences scarred her.

Of all three kids, Kathy bore the deepest wounds from that period of instability. The coping mechanisms she mimicked from me demanded constant adaptation as she matured. Our unspoken traumas left indelible marks on her psyche that I was too close to fully recognize.

My daughters circled back to provide support as my second husband's valiant battle against brain cancer intensified. The hospital became a second home to us all. As one child returned home, the other succumbed, forcing us into the dizzying vortex of grief once more.

My beautiful daughters stayed pillars of strength when I had none left. After the dust settled from the chaos, Laurie returned to school in Maryland. But stalwart Kathy remained steadfast at my side when I needed her most.

What I failed to notice beneath her rock-solid exterior was a daughter barely holding herself together. Kathy's silent struggles demanded more care and attention than I could muster in my own fog of mourning. Our shared grief sent us reeling down different paths. There's no doubt in my mind that Kathy was still feeling the unresolved pain of her father's absence 12 years earlier.

While her selflessness in caring for me never wavered, Kathy grappled alone with feelings of insecurity and loss. Consumed with holding my own world together, I overlooked her unspoken vulnerability.

My blind spot as a mother haunts me now. Kathy shouldered far too much without complaint, bottling up inner turmoil to prioritize my stability. If only I had stopped to truly see the scared little girl hiding behind the facade of the strong woman. There is so much I would change if I could live those difficult days again.

But time only flows in one direction. The solace I find lies in knowing Kathy's spirit soars unfettered now by the burdens she carried silently for too long. Her memory lives on, reminding me there is always more beneath the surface than meets the eye. My daughter, now my angel, will remain my guiding light - illuminating the shadows and reflecting back the love that flows between a mother and child eternally.

Recalling Kathy's Marriage To Ron

When Kathy's father left, I felt she just wanted to be in a place where she felt loved and needed. A kind of security that would make her feel comfortable and relaxed. When she met Ron, he obviously made her feel that comfort. His stability seemed like a life raft in her stormy seas of loss. Trusting him wholeheartedly, she embarked on a new chapter, leaving the familiar shelter of our family home to build a life with him in Miami.

The allure of a steady career and financial independence beckoned Kathy. Her savvy in corporate travel, honed over years in our family business, opened doors to promising opportunities. Before long, she was managing travel for a major company, reaping rewards both professional and personal. Her competence proved invaluable in an industry she knew inside and out.

A comfortable retirement seemed assured, the light at the end of the tunnel after years of tireless work. Kathy had fought through emotional turmoil to secure this stable future for herself. I could not have been more proud of her resilience and tenacity.

Yet her personal life with Ron had weathered its share of unfortunate storms. Their marriage ebbed and flowed, punctuated by moments of fracture and reconciliation. Though I harbored reservations about Ron from the beginning, what mattered most was my daughter's happiness. If he brought her joy and peace of mind, that outweighed any lingering doubts.

Over time spent together in Miami, I noticed subtle but troubling shifts in Kathy's demeanor. A once lively woman seemed to embrace a more subdued presence. The changes were gradual, an almost imperceptible metamorphosis. As her mother, red flags rose in my mind but I hesitated to pry without cause.

Sensing something amiss, I ventured to ask if she was truly alright. Kathy assured me all was well, that these changes were just part of life's natural ebb and flow. Trusting her words, I tamped down the worries simmering below the surface.

Looking back, I can identify the moment that marked the beginning of the major shift in Kathy's marriage. It coincided with her decision to move with Ron from Miami to Homestead full-time. But their fresh start failed to provide the peace they sought. Removing herself from the job and life she loved proved difficult for Kathy. Being isolated in a small town miles from family took an incremental toll on her spirit. Ron grew ever more consumed by his need for control and security. Kathy confided that he seemed to find distress around every corner, reacting to even minor issues with irrational anger. She adapted and walked on eggshells to avoid triggering his temper.

I suspected Ron's rigid personality and volatility presented deeper issues than Kathy let on. But my gentle probing was met with platitudes that all marriages have ups and downs. She assured me not to worry, though her eyes whispered volumes she could not say out loud. My mother's intuition sensed a shift from occasional marital spats into something more ominously controlling.

Ron became consumed by troubling conspiracy theories, isolating himself for hours online or on the phone espousing wild dangers no one else could see. Kathy revealed very little of what she endured, but I could read between the lines well enough to know she was carrying a heavy burden largely alone. When I pressed the issue pointedly during a visit, fear flashed across her face. She changed the subject, making it clear any intervention on my part would only drive her away.

And so I was forced to watch silently from a distance as my once fiery, independent daughter slowly became a ghost of her former self. Ron's irrationality and volatility increased, yet Kathy remained doggedly devoted to him. She accepted the bars of her gilded cage, resigning herself to a life lived walking on eggshells.

I longed to shelter Kathy from the gathering storm, but she made it abundantly clear she would not leave Ron. Cut off from resources, she was wholly dependent on him. Though every protective maternal instinct screamed for me to intervene, Kathy refused any lifeline that could be seen as criticism of her husband. She further isolated herself to avoid outside "meddling" that might rock their teetering boat.

My heart ached watching her light dimmed by the day. But my hands were painfully tied by a loyal daughter's pleas. Kathy clung stubbornly to the belief that her place was by her husband's side, for better or worse. I could only hope and pray she would reach her limit. That one day she would walk through my door, ready to start a new chapter away from Ron's darkness.

Of course, that day never came. Kathy's story ended abrasively, leaving me awash in regrets for not taking a stand sooner. For failing to push past her walls of false assurances. For not trusting my intuition that a deeper evil lurked beneath the surface of their lives.

But the path of guilt leads nowhere good. I know Kathy does not blame me, wherever she is now. Her eternal light shines on, guiding me to make peace with the past. All I can do is carry her in my heart and trust that she rests in the arms of angels now. No more walking on eggshells, no more silent suffering. Just everlasting peace for my precious daughter. That truth alone comforts me and gives me strength to carry on.

The Silent Struggles: Unveiling Kathy's Pain

My journey with trust has been a winding road, stemming from the earliest days of my first marriage and growing ever more complicated as life unfolded. Caution became my constant companion, and I found myself perpetually guarded, unwilling to fully open up to anyone. Yet, drowning in self-pity was never an option—I simply couldn't afford the luxury of wallowing. I harbored no negative attitudes; the mere thought of failure never crossed my mind. Thank goodness for that unwavering determination.

Reflecting on my daughter, Kathy, I couldn't help but recognize her resemblance to me in many ways. There were moments of self-blame, wondering why I hadn't seen her distress earlier and reached out to her. Her burden must have been unimaginable. Now, as illness encroached upon her, she must have sensed that something was terribly wrong. Perhaps, in her heart, she wished that mere optimism could remedy everything. It became painfully apparent that her husband wasn't someone she could confide in. I pondered how long she had been living in such conditions.

During my visit in February, immediately following my son's funeral, the sight of Kathy left me utterly shocked. Her husband picked me up from the airport, and the drive to their home in Homestead was filled with a haunting silence. Kathy had purchased the townhouse they resided in after divorcing him in 2014. Initially an investment, she had transformed it into a beautiful sanctuary after they remarried, infusing every corner with her exquisite taste in decor.

Arriving at the townhouse, my heart plummeted at the sight of her. She seemed so frail, so fragile. Every fiber of my being wanted to convince her to come home with me, to seek the help she so desperately needed. However, her determination to retire first and then seek respite at my home prevailed. I deeply regret listening to her and not insisting that she return with me. There's a profound sense that she might still be alive today if only she had come back with me. The weight of that decision weighs heavily upon my heart

Walking into her house, problems seemed to hang heavy in the air. The closed blinds, shutting out the vibrant Florida sunshine, immediately caught my attention. It felt as though a barrier had been erected, severing any connection to the outside world. The somber ambiance within echoed an overwhelming sense of depression. My gut instincts, unfortunately, were spot on. The signs were all there: constant pain etched onto her face, once radiant but now devoid of any traces of smiles. She appeared painfully thin, her lack of appetite a telling sign that all was not well in this household. The fatigue etched in her eyes and defeated posture only added to the grim picture. And there he sat, her husband, with scant empathy for the woman who had been his unwavering support. His explosive temper was on full display, a stark contrast to the heartbreaking situation. Witnessing it all shattered my heart into a million pieces.

Numbness had settled in after just losing her brother, and now, seeing my daughter in such a state was unbearable. The thought of losing her, too, was a chilling prospect I couldn't fathom.

Amid the chaos of the Covid pandemic, DelMonte had

graciously allowed her to work remotely from home. Her makeshift workspace was arranged at the table in the breakfast nook, where each morning, she'd start her day with a cup of coffee, delving into the demanding world of the travel business. Her expertise in her field was undeniable. Amidst her busy schedule, we stole moments to chat, sharing precious breaks that allowed us to connect. Simply being in the same room with her filled me with joy. We discussed her retirement dreams and cherished plans for spending time together. Conversations also drifted to her brother, and she expressed deep regret about missing his funeral. Their bond had been unbreakable since the day I brought him home from the hospital.

Throughout my stay, Ron, her husband, remained glued to the porch from sunrise till nightfall—smoking, drinking beer, and fixated on the television. Despite being within earshot of our conversations, he never once engaged, maintaining a conspicuous distance. It was evident that my presence was solely for Kathy, and as far as he was concerned, his demeanor remained unchanged—aloof and distant, just as before. This time was no different, a stark testament to his detachment from the situation.

I held her tightly in my arms, cherishing our final goodbye as I planted a kiss on her sweet, precious face. Departing, I carried a weight of worries about her well-being, little knowing it would mark the last time our eyes met in this world. I pleaded with her to promise me she'd see a doctor. Sadly, that was a promise she couldn't fulfill.

Even now, I grapple with regrets about not staying longer, not probing further into her health. A dear friend comforted me, insisting it was her husband's responsibility, not mine. But my advice to all parents stands firm: pay heed to what you observe and hear, regardless of age, and do everything within your power to shield your children. Kathy remained oblivious to the grave jeopardy her health was in. She held onto hope for recovery and the enjoyment of her retirement. Diabetes plays tricks on the mind, and it was astonishing how she managed to navigate her job despite her condition.

That friend was right in guiding me away from dwelling on helping my daughter. I discovered the painful reality that I had no rights as a parent; when you're married, your spouse holds all the control. I had to grapple with his evasive "I don't know" responses. However, upon his passing two months later, I stepped into the role of her next of kin, finally gaining the authority to request all her records. That marked the start of my quest for every piece of information available, a quest seeking answers to the tragic mystery of my daughter's untimely passing.

When the news of Kathy's demise reached us, my daughter, her husband Tom, and I united to plan her funeral. Ron seemed lost and incapable of navigating the arrangements, so we took charge. At the time of Kathy's passing, Ron hadn't been diagnosed with cancer, though his declining health was evident. His family relocated him to a nearby nursing home, where he was eventually diagnosed with colon cancer. Just two months after Kathy's passing, Ron also bid farewell to this world.

Following Kathy's Funeral Mass, the Smith family convened for a dinner gathering, a time for relatives to share stories and memories. While it was a pleasant event, I found myself needing a quiet refuge to wrestle with the depth of my sorrow. Amidst the laughter and conversations, I sought solace—a place to let the tears stream and my heart grapple with the overwhelming grief. The reality of what had occurred was beyond my comprehension, and solitude was essential for me to process the painful loss of my dear daughter.

At the dinner table, I sat across from Ron, Kathy's husband. His unexpected words pierced through the din, *"I want you to have Kathy's ashes."* Shock coursed through me, leaving me speechless. I urged him to reconsider, but he had already made up his mind. Gratefully, albeit with confusion swirling within, I accepted his gesture. I resolved to bury Kathy and John, my son, together. His response was a simple "fine," leaving the decision in my hands. I still ponder his motives, though I refrain from questioning his choice. The opportunity to lay my daughter and son to rest side by side feels like a blessing amidst the abyss of these colossal losses. Yet, the pain remains, the greatest I've ever endured. I've made peace with my son's passing, having done all I could, but the circumstances surrounding my daughter's demise leave me yearning for answers.

Soon after Kathy's passing, Ron and his brother swiftly took charge of her assets. My investigation revealed their expedient visits to Kathy's workplace, presumably for insurance and retirement funds. Shockingly, we were left uninformed and bereft of a single cent from her estate. They remained resolutely tight-lipped, exacerbating our distress. Upon Ron's passing, the townhouse—Kathy's former residence—was promptly put up for sale without a word to us. The sole beneficiary of these proceedings was Mary Lynn, Ron's mother. Losing my daughter was agonizing enough, but the added financial implications exacerbated the pain. While such situations might be expected under normal circumstances, the swift turn of events, coupled with what I perceive as neglectful behavior on her husband's part, makes it excruciatingly hard to accept.

I held onto the hope that they would eventually do the right thing. The fact that they didn't even engage in a discussion about it left me astounded and in disbelief. They, too, had lost a son and brother. Couldn't they empathize with the anguish we were enduring? Understanding their acceptance of this whole situation has been an insurmountable challenge for me.

Echoes of Grief

In the throes of grief, I found myself unable to think clearly. I was unaware of my rights or Kathy's in the midst of this situation. I didn't know where to seek help or guidance. My love for my daughter fueled a burning desire for justice on her behalf. It might be an arduous journey, but I was resolute—determined to amplify her silenced voice. Her life wouldn't be in vain. I'm convinced she'll always be with us in spirit, inspiring me to tirelessly work towards ensuring others learn from the heartbreaking experience we've endured.

Throughout my life, I've witnessed countless miracles. Where would I be today without those moments of Divine Intervention? As I grow older, I find myself drawing closer to Almighty God, who continues to bless me and my family with unwavering faith, courage, love, and resilience. I can't envision life without faith and a steadfast commitment to doing what's morally right.

January 13, 2023, marked a year since John's passing. I spent that January in Niceville, Florida, reconnecting with friends. While it was good to be back, I also missed my family in Delaware. Life was evolving, and I was adapting to the changes. However, in April, I experienced a heart attack that compelled me to slow down, manage stress, and learn the art of relaxation. Despite this, I found joy in the visits from my grandchildren and the pleasant weather in Delaware.

Every year, my siblings and their families gather for a reunion in Wisconsin, at the homestead where I grew up. This cherished property has been in our family for over a century, a place where my father spent his childhood. The invitation extended to family and friends brought together relatives I had never met before. Now, the younger generation—my nieces and nephews—have taken charge of organizing these gatherings, and their efforts were truly remarkable.

Laurie and I made the heartfelt decision that Kathy and John should rest alongside our departed family members. Arranging for their burial during our family reunion in Wisconsin seemed fitting and appropriate.

The family reunion, set for Saturday, preceded the burial planned for the following Monday. The journey from Delaware to Wisconsin was too strenuous for me, so Laurie and Tom dropped me off at the Philadelphia airport to fly while they continued by road with Kathy and John's ashes.

On Monday, August 5, 2023, a serene graveside ceremony took place, laying both my children to rest beside my parents and other cherished family members. It was a moment of deep sorrow yet accompanied by a sense of solace. In an ideal world, this isn't how families should come together. My siblings and I stood side by side, grieving grandparents, burying two beloved children—a heart-wrenching reality. I stayed an additional week to share precious moments with my family. The final days were spent in Milwaukee, where my sister Dee, also a widow, provided comfort amidst the anguish of loss.

After that, I returned to Delaware, aiming to sit down and assimilate the happenings of the tumultuous year that was 2022. Uncertain about how I would move forward with my life, one thing was clear: moving to Delaware in September, to be closer to Laurie, Tom, and my grandchildren, was unequivocally the right decision for me.

My communication with Kathy's in-laws was scarce, almost nonexistent. Despite the absence of direct answers, I persisted in my pursuit to uncover the circumstances surrounding Kathy's tragic passing. The pivotal figure who held the key to these answers, her husband, was no longer present, but that didn't deter my quest for the truth. I delved into the hospital records and meticulously went through the ambulance report. Each page I read felt like an emotional ordeal, yet I persevered through the torment.

The harrowing truth emerged: my daughter lay on the floor for a harrowing 24 hours before her husband finally made the distressing call to 911.

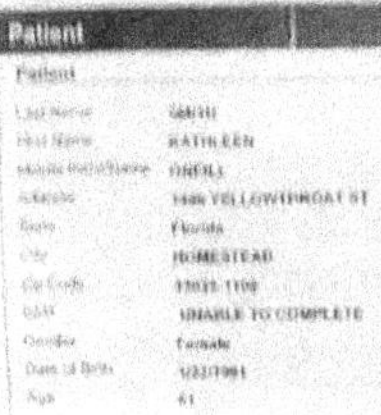
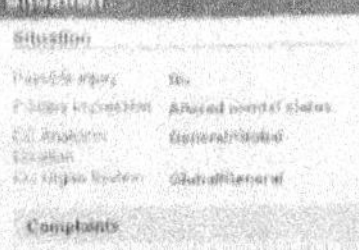
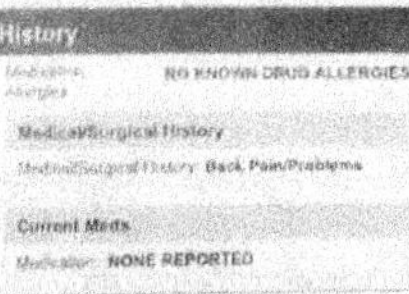

Miami-Dade Fire Rescue

Incident: 2220610
Patient: SMITH, KATHLEEN ONEILL
Impression: Altered mental status
Case Status: CLOSED

Patient

Last Name	SMITH
First Name	KATHLEEN
Middle Initial/Name	ONEILL
Address	1446 YELLOWTHROAT ST
State	Florida
City	HOMESTEAD
Zip Code	33035-1109
SSN	UNABLE TO COMPLETE
Gender	Female
Date of Birth	1/23/1961
Age	61
Age Units	Years

Situation

Possible Injury	No
Primary Impression	Altered mental status
Call Location	General/Global

Complaints

Complaint: Hypertensive Type: Chief (Primary)
Duration: 1 Time Units: Days

Symptoms

Indication: Weakness

History

Medications Allergies: NO KNOWN DRUG ALLERGIES

Medical/Surgical History

Medical/Surgical History: Back Pain/Problems

Current Meds

Medication: NONE REPORTED

Patient Transfer

Transport From/Unit	L68
Transfer Date	08/14/2022 20:44
Summary of This Care	08/14/2022 20:29 Patient Assessment

08/14/2022 20:29: Vitals [BP Systolic: 60] [BP Diastolic: 40] [BP Orthostatic: Lying] [BP Method: Cuff-Manual Auscultated] [Heart Rate: 70] [Heart Rate Method: Electronic Monitor - Pulse Oximeter] [Pulse Oximetry: 96] [Pulse Rhythm: Regular] [Respiratory Rate: 14] [Respiratory Effort: Normal] [Blood Glucose Level: 463] [Eye: 4: Opens Eyes spontaneously] [Verbal: 4: Confused, Cries but consolable, inappropriate interactions] [Motor: 5: Localizing pain] [Total GCS: 13]

Narrative: Pt fell a day go and has been on the floor since. Pt is lethargic and slow to answer and follow commands. Pt is hypotensive 60/40 Pts vital signs are

Narrative

Pt husband complained of pt having weakness for one day. Pt was on the ground and did not have strength to stand up. Upon assessment, pt was hypotensive and hyperglycemic. Pt denied chest pain, shortness of breath, stomach pain, loss of consciousness, blurred vision.

Pt GCS of 15. No deficits noted. No neurological deficits noted.

Exam, IV, EKG, normal saline. Pt was transported to Homestead hospital for further medical evaluation.

Patient Care Report

Miami-Dade Fire Rescue
9300 NW 41st Street, Doral, Florida 33178
Official Document

Incident: 2220619
Patient: SMITH, KATHLEEN ONEILL
Impression: Altered mental status
Care Status: CLOSED

Care Events		
Date/Time	Event	Details
2022-09-14 20:42:10	Vitals	Heart Rate: 70 Pulse Rhythm: Regular Heart Rate Method: Palpated Respiratory Rate: 18 Respiratory Effort: Normal BP Method: Cuff-Manual Auscultated BP Systolic: 83 BP Diastolic: 40 Blood Glucose Level: 483 Pulse Oximetry: 98 Pulse Oximetry Status: Room Air End Tidal Carbon Dioxide (ETCO2): 14 Eye: 4: Opens Eyes spontaneously Verbal: 5: Oriented, Smiles, Follows objects, Interacts Motor: 6: Obeys commands, Appropriate response to stimulation Total GCS: 15
2022-09-14 20:42:13	Patient Assessment	Crew ID: Garcia, Frank
2022-09-14 20:51:27	Normal saline	Dose Units: Milliliters (ml) Dosage: 200.000 Route: Intravenous (IV) Crew ID: Samy, Olivier
2022-09-14 20:51:36	IV (Extremity)	Site: Forearm-Right Equipment Size: 20G Catheter Attempts: 1 Successful: Yes Secured Via: Veni Guard Crew ID: Samy, Olivier Condition upon release: Patient with no signs of infiltration
2022-09-14 20:52:13	12 Lead ECG Obtained	Resulting Rhythm: Sinus Rhythm Crew ID: Garcia, Frank
2022-09-14 20:59:39	Vitals	Heart Rate: 76 Pulse Rhythm: Regular Heart Rate Method: Electronic Monitor - Pulse Oximeter Respiratory Rate: 12 Respiratory Effort: Normal BP Method: Cuff-Manual Auscultated BP Systolic: 88 BP Diastolic: 52 Pulse Oximetry: 99 Pulse Oximetry Status: Room Air Eye: 4: Opens Eyes spontaneously Verbal: 5: Oriented, Smiles, Follows objects, Interacts Motor: 6: Obeys commands, Appropriate response to stimulation Total GCS: 15
2022-09-14 21:00:44	Oxygen	Dose Units: Liters Per Minute (LPM (gas)) Dosage: 15.000 Route: Non-Rebreather Mask Crew ID: Samy, Olivier

Name
ID:
Patient ID: 091422204941
Incident ID:
Age: 61   Sex: F

12-Lead
9/14/2022
PR 0.176s
QT/QTc
P QRS-T Axes
aVR

HR 70bpm Abnormal ECG **Unconfirmed**
8:52:32 PM Sinus rhythm
QRS 0.126s Possible inferior infarct - age undetermined
0.462/0.479s Lateral T wave abnormality is nonspecific
73\69\86

x1.0 .05-150Hz 25mm/sec
Physio-Control, Inc.   Comments:

R77 MDFR 3313494-011 LP1549455024

CERTIFIED TRUE COPY of electronic record maintained by Miami-Dade Fire Rescue Department 9300 NW 41 Street, Doral FL 33178 Central Records Bureau
Records Custodian: _______________

Patient Care Report

Page 3 of 6

Miami-Dade Fire Rescue
6300 NW 47th Street, Doral, Florida 33178
Official Document

Incident:
Patient: SMITH, KATHLEEN OMEGA
Impression: Hypoglycemia
Case Status: CLOSED

Exam

Patient Position as Found: Lying on Back
Coronavirus Disease 2019 (COVID-19) Assessment: None
COVID-19 Assessment Results: Patient DOES NOT meet Suspected COVID-19 criteria

Date/Time	Assessments	Comments
2022-09-14 20:34:23	Mental Status: Responds to Voice	
	Skin: Normal	
	Neurological: Not Done	
	Head: Normal	
	Face: Normal	
	Neck: Normal	
	Chest/Lungs: Normal	
	Pelvis/Genitourinary: Normal	
	Eyes: Bilateral Normal (Reactive)	
	Spine: Back of normal Normal	
	Extremities: GMC x4	
	Abdomen: Generalized Normal	

Care Events

Date/Time	Event	Details
2022-09-14 20:26:01	Patient Assessment	Primary Survey: None
2022-09-14 20:34:44	Vitals	Heart Rate: 78 Transmission: Regular Method: Manual Electronic Monitor; Pulse Oximeter Respiratory Rate: 24; Respiration Effort Normal Method: CPAP through a nasal cannula BP System; BP Systolic: 88 BP Diastolic: 48; GCS: Verbal: 4 Eyes: 4 Motor: 6; Blood Glucose Level: 553 Pupils: Normal; 98 Pulse Oximetry SpO2 Report for Pain: 0; Dyspnea Signs Auscultation/Lung Sounds: 4; Confused; Cries but consolable, inappropriate interactions Weight: 6; Localizes pain Total SpO2: 93
2022-09-14 20:47:44	IV (Extremity)	Site: Forearm Right Equipment Size: 20G Catheter Attempts: 1 Successful; No Flow IV: Gauge rates, Clinician

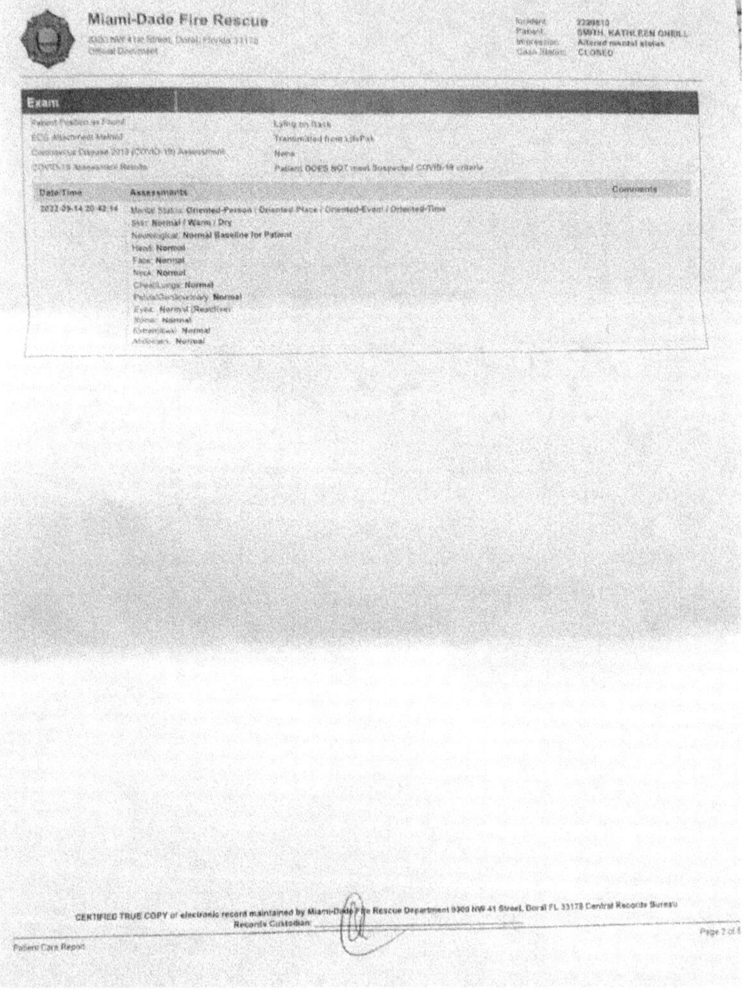

Miami-Dade Fire Rescue
9300 NW 41st Street, Doral, Florida 33178
Official Document

Incident: 2228810
Patient: SMITH, KATHLEEN ONEILL
Impression: Altered mental status
Case Status: CLOSED

Exam

Patient Position as Found	Lying on Back
ECG Attachment Method	Transmitted from LifePak
Coronavirus Disease 2019 (COVID-19) Assessment	None
COVID-19 Assessment Results	Patient DOES NOT meet Suspected COVID-19 criteria

Date/Time	Assessments	Comments
2022-09-14 20:42:14	Mental Status: Oriented-Person / Oriented-Place / Oriented-Event / Oriented-Time Skin: Normal / Warm / Dry Neurological: Normal Baseline for Patient Head: Normal Face: Normal Neck: Normal Chest/Lungs: Normal Pelvis/Genitourinary: Normal Eyes: Normal (Reaction) Nose: Normal Extremities: Normal Abdomen: Normal	

CERTIFIED TRUE COPY of electronic record maintained by Miami-Dade Fire Rescue Department 9300 NW 41 Street, Doral FL 33178 Central Records Bureau
Records Custodian:

Patient Care Report

Page 2 of 6

The hospital records revealed images of her frail, bruised 100-pound body—a haunting sight etched into my memory forever. His assertion that she had been taken to the hospital on the night before her death was contradicted by a friend of Kathy's. Upon obtaining the hospital report, it was painfully evident that Kathy had been hospitalized for at least a couple of days—a fact he concealed.

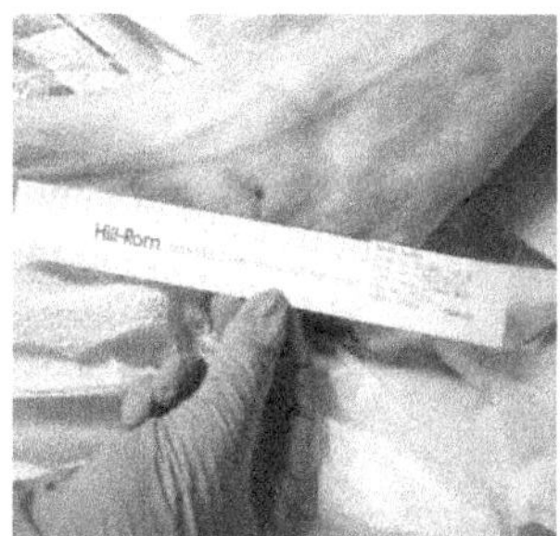
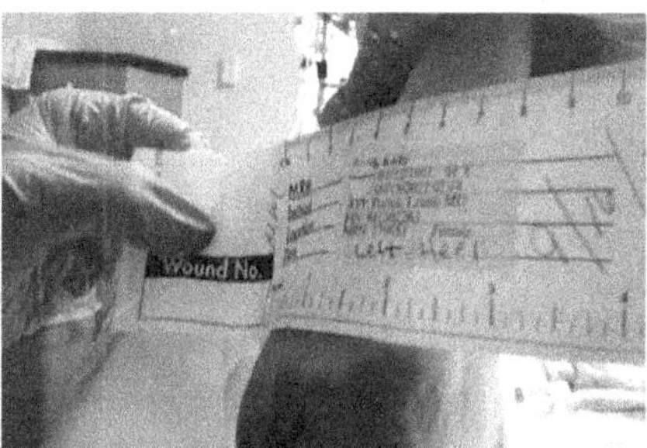
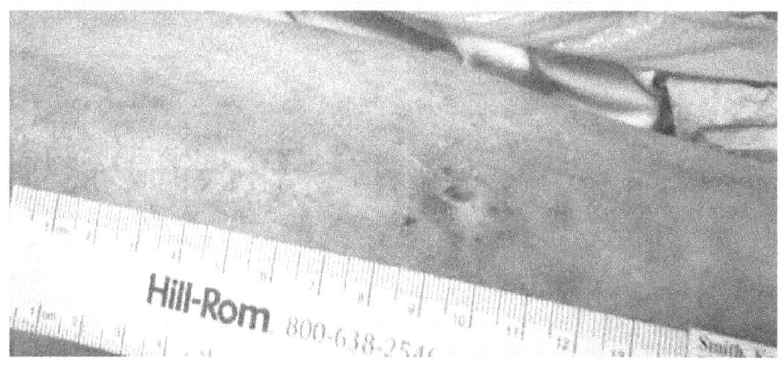

There was no call made to notify her mother or sister during those critical hours. Had we been informed, we would have had ample time to be by her side. The hospital documents furnished answers, but they also raised an alarming question that relentlessly plagues me: Why didn't he summon an ambulance when she fell? He, more than anyone, knew her fragility. The delay in seeking medical help in the face of her low blood sugar remains incomprehensible and senseless to me.

Patient Name: Smith, Kathy
MRN: 179651   Admit Date: 9/14/2022
Encounter: 941302263   Discharge Date: 9/16/2022

Consultation Notes

Document Type: Critical Care Consultation
Service Date/Time: 9/15/2022 08:00 EDT
Result Status: Auth (Verified)
Document Subject: Critical Care Consult Note
Perform Information: Lopetegui,Juan Antonio MD (9/15/2022 12:14 EDT)
Sign Information: Lopetegui,Juan Antonio MD (9/15/2022 12:14 EDT)

Chief Complaint
PT FOUND ON FLOOR BELIEVED MORE THAN 24 HRS DRIINKING, HUSBAND CALLED
911 PT HYPOTENSIVE 60/40 NS GIVEN 500. BGL 463.

Referring Physician
Portes MD

Reason for Consultation
Acute respiratory failure
Diabetic ketoacidosis

HPI
61 years old female patient, background of diabetes mellitus, brought to the emergency
room after being found lying on the floor, febrile and hypotensive and pink by
EMS, upon arrival to the ER blood pressure 100/66, no fever, oximetry 100% on a
nonrebreather mask. Patient had to be intubated, admitted to ICU with diagnosis of
diabetic ketoacidosis, high anion gap metabolic acidemia, acute respiratory
failure shock dependent on a norepinephrine drip.

ROS
Unable to obtain

Physical Exam

Vitals & Measurements
T: 36.6 °C (Oral) HR: 104 (Peripheral) HR: 110 (Monitored) RR: 28
RR: 29 (Total) BP: 106/59 SpO2: 100% HT: 160 cm WT: 55 kg (Measured)
BMI: 21.48 BMI: 17.21
General: [sedated, well nourished, no acute distress]
Eye: [Pupils equal, EOMI, normal conjunctiva]
ENMT : [Normocephalic,, ears/nose inspection non-revealing, moist oral mucosa, no
scleral icterus, no sinus tenderness]
Neck: [Supple, non-tender, trachea midline, no thyroid enlargement or tenderness]
Respiratory : [Intubated,normal respiratory effort, clear to auscultation]
Cardiovascular: [Regular rate and rhythm, no murmur or pedal edema]
Gastrointestinal: [Soft, non-tender, non-distended, normal bowel sounds, no masses, no
hepatomegaly]
Musculoskeletal: [No digital clubbing or cyanosis,]
Skin: [Skin is warm, no rashes or lesions]
Neurologic: [sedated

Clinical Images
Reviewed by me

Assessment/Plan
61 years old female patient admitted to ICU with diagnosis of acute respiratory failure,
shock, diabetic ketoacidosis.
Plan:
Fluid resuscitation
Insulin drip
Replace electrolytes

Problem List/Past Medical History
Ongoing
   No qualifying data

Procedure/Surgical History
Negative

Medications
Medications (23) Active
Scheduled: (8)
chlorhexidine 2% topical wipe 1 EA,
Topical, Daily
diazePAM (Valium) 10 mg/2 mL syringe
 5 mg 1 mL, IV Push, Daily
enoxaparin (Lovenox) 40 mg/0.4 mL
syringe 40 mg 0.4 mL, SubCutaneous,
Daily
famotidine (Pepcid) PF 20 mg/2 mL vial
 20 mg 2 mL, IV Push, Daily
mupirocin (Bactroban) 2% topical
ointment 22 g 1 appl, Nasal, BID
potassium chloride 20 mEq oral powder
packet 20 mEq 1 packets, Nasoduodenal
Tube, Daily
thiamine 200 mg 2 mL, IV Piggyback,
Every 8 hrs
thiamine 100 mg tablet 200 mg 2 tab(s),
Nasoduodenal Tube, Daily
Continuous: (10)
dextrose 10% 981 mL + sodium
chloride 77 mEq 981 mL, IV Continuous,
200 mL/hr
dextrose 5%-Sodium Chloride 0.45%
1,000 mL + potassium chloride 20 mEq
+ potassium phosphate 10 mmo 1,000
mL, IV Continuous, 150 mL/hr
fentaNYL. 2,500 mcg [25 mcg/hr] +
Premix 50 mL 50 mL, IV Continuous, 0.5
mL/hr
insulin regular 100 units [12 units/hr]
+ sodium chloride 0.9% 99 mL 99 mL,
IV Continuous, 12 mL/hr
lactated ringers 1,000 mL 1,000 mL, IV
Continuous, 125 mL/hr
norepinephrine/NaCl 0.9% 16 mg [2
mcg/min] + Premix Sodium Chloride
0.9% 250 mL 250 mL, IV Continuous, 1.88
mL/hr

Report ID: 626004943   Page 62 of 706   Print Date/Time: 4/11/2023 12:30 EDT

Reflecting on December 2019, when Kathy visited alone to celebrate my birthday and spend time with her brother, a jarring memory surfaces. I vividly recall being taken aback by her significant weight loss and expressing my concern. Her response – "Mom, I'm not trying to lose weight. It's just coming off."— left me unsettled. Despite the reassurance, I couldn't shake off a lingering unease. She seemed to eat normally in my presence, and her conscientiousness about her weight led me to believe this was another phase for her.

We shared such delightful moments together during her visit—it was a treasure trove of laughter and fond memories. Watching her and her brother reminisce and share hearty laughs was akin to a rejuvenating balm for the soul. After many years of tending to caregiving duties, this infusion of laughter felt like sunshine flooding into my soul. Yet, the time flew by too swiftly. To add to my 80th birthday celebration, my grandson joined us in Florida, enriching the festivities and filling my heart and soul with immeasurable joy.

During her visit, I couldn't help but wonder why her husband hadn't accompanied her. I inquired about it, and she mentioned that he had gone to Tampa to visit his family and she planned to meet him there after leaving me. Despite some inner concerns, I was so elated to have her undivided company that I chose to overlook any red flags.

Then, the shadow of the pandemic loomed over our lives. Covid struck in January 2020, plunging the country into disarray and instilling a pervasive sense of fear. Kathy, like everyone else, was ensnared in this environment of uncertainty and fear that seemed never-ending.

Amidst the chaos, Kathy's workplace took precautions to

safeguard their employees. They facilitated her working from home, providing her with the tools she needed—a computer— to manage travel bookings and necessary reports. It was a commendable setup for her in those trying times.

Despite being immersed in the travel industry, she had no inclination to travel herself. Her pleasures lay in the simpler aspects of life—home, family, flowers, and the occasional shopping trip. Kathy relished the company of others and was known for her dedication and hard work.

As Covid gripped our lives, our travel plans came to an abrupt halt. The pandemic dictated that I couldn't have visitors over or venture out due to the risk of John falling ill. Navigating his doctor appointments was a daunting task initially, but I gradually eased my fears, taking prudent precautions to ensure our safety.

The persisting fear seemed to cast a perpetual shadow over Kathy's life. She chose to retreat behind closed doors, isolating herself from the world outside. It was evident that this fear played a pivotal role in deterring her from seeking medical attention. Ron, her husband, repeatedly mentioned his struggle in convincing her to visit a doctor. Despite having been generally healthy, the prospect of dealing with a doctor was entirely new and unsettling for her. Her unwavering focus on retirement seemed to eclipse her instincts to prioritize her health. However, I remained steadfast in urging her to prioritize a doctor's appointment.

In my understanding, a fundamental aspect of a close marital relationship involves supporting each other's well-being. However, instead of a concerted effort to address Kathy's health concerns, all I encountered was a resounding echo of "she won't go to the doctor." I even suggested to Ron that Kathy might be diabetic, a condition that could be managed if detected early.

Reflecting on the situation, I wish I could turn back time and rewrite this whole narrative. Kathy needed someone to guide her, someone to protect and care for her. This remains my deepest regret. If Ron couldn't fulfill this role, I could have stepped in. There was so much I didn't know then, and I learned so much more after it was already too late. It's agonizing to think that I was deprived of holding her hand during her last days. I brought her into this world, yet I wasn't there when she departed. My beautiful firstborn daughter left this world without her husband by her side, and that will forever weigh heavily on my heart.

The Silence of Smith Family

The pain of losing a loved one is a wound that often remains open. In my pursuit of closure and answers surrounding the tragic passing of my daughter Kathy, I was met with silence and evasion from those who were once considered family. My attempt to reach out and discuss matters pertaining to Kathy's assets and the circumstances leading to her death was met with a singular, lengthy conversation from Ron's brother, Robert. Instead of discussing the critical aspects related to Kathy's passing, the conversation gravitated towards praising Ron and their purportedly blissful marriage.

There was no acknowledgment or discussion of settling Kathy's assets, the extent of their collection, or the unfortunate events that led to Kathy lying unattended for 24 hours before the ambulance was called. I was inundated with excuses, none of which provided any solace or resonated with the depth of my grief. It became apparent that their actions failed to align with the love and respect they professed for Kathy.

It felt disheartening to witness the lack of empathy and understanding from individuals who claimed to have cherished Kathy deeply. If their love for her were genuine, they would have recognized the emotional distress caused by their actions and attempted to rectify the situation, especially considering the uncertain circumstances surrounding Kathy's passing.

Their avoidance of a fair and equitable resolution is a constant source of anguish. It reflects a lack of regard for Kathy's memory and disrespect for her family. This treatment further deepens my disappointment in humanity. Even amidst their professed happiness, they failed to acknowledge Kathy's distress and needs during a time when her well-being hung in the balance.

The forwarded message below encapsulates my attempt to find answers and closure, an endeavor met with avoidance and an unwillingness to engage in resolving these matters. It is a reflection of the silence and lack of empathy that echoes through this ordeal, underscoring my desperate search for justice and peace in the wake of Kathy's untimely departure.

****

From: Jean Thomson

Date: March 17, 2023 at 9:03:59 PM EDT

To: The Smith Family ... Marylynn, Robert, Robbie, Rebecca

<u>Subject: Kathy's Mother/looking for answers</u>

"I'm writing this letter with the hope that expressing all that has kept me up at night for the last 6 months, I might find rest and peace. It's been 6 months since my precious daughter, Kathy, passed...over 37 of her 61 years spent with Ron. He was a part of our family as well during that time. Since her death, my mind has been filled with questions on several levels and I'm hoping you can offer insight.

I never interfered with Kathy and Ron's marriage but always worried about her. Two separations and a divorce does not indicate a happy marriage. The last time I saw Kathy was February 2022, right after my son died. The whole time I was there, I saw no affection between her and Ron. It made me wonder why they were together. Sad! Ron looked well then... sat on the porch and smoked and drank beer... but Kathy was obviously struggling with her health. I am now left with questions as to what happened to my daughter that she died just 7 months later. Anytime I asked Ron about details surrounding her death, which I did several times, he always responded that he didn't know and seemed to be irritated at me for even asking. I want to know how many times did she fall the day before or the day of her passing? What time of day was it? Did Ron have any conversation with her? Did he go about his day while Kathy lay on the floor? How long before the ambulance was called? What time was she admitted to the emergency room? As sick as she was, why did he leave her side at the hospital to let her die alone? Why didn't he remain with her knowing she was in critical condition.... and at least hold her hand? He didn't call me when she was admitted to the hospital or when she died. It was my daughter, Laurie, who called and gave me this horrific news. If you can answer any of these questions, I would be so very grateful.

Kathy worked hard all her life and through her job, provided health insurance for her and Ron, as well as financial stability with the many years she worked in travel and for DelMonte, saving up stock etc., for her upcoming retirement. I recently discovered that Ron had filed bankruptcy at some point for his business, and to my knowledge, other than social security, had no other financial contributions. It seems, from any objective observer, that the assets, insurance money, stocks, 401 retirement account, the townhouse they were living in, and which she purchased while divorced from Ron, were pretty much Kathy's hard work, responsibility, and exemplary work ethics.

Thus, I have a hard time coming to terms with the fact that the result of all my daughter's hard work goes solely to benefit your family, especially since Ron passed so soon after Kathy, and also knowing that Kathy would not have wanted it that way. This does not seem right or fair. In February 2022, when I was visiting her, I had gifted her 100 shares of Apple stock which is now worth about $17,000.00. Why should this go to your family instead of my own family?

I want to make it clear that I do not need the money. I too have worked hard all my life and enjoy financial stability as a result, but I haven't been able to reconcile how your family can in good conscience accept all these "gifts" and good fortune without consideration of Kathy's family.

The marriage, deaths, lack of child heirs and the whole situation is highly unusual and unique which then "requires "people of good will to take all of that into consideration and find an equitable solution. At the very least, keep Kathy's family apprised of what is going on with the estate settlement. The silence and lack of communication indicates to me that you probably know all of this.

I took some time to decide whether or not to write this letter as I realize it may sound harsh, but after much prayer and consideration, I feel strongly that it needs to be said for my sake as well as yours, and perhaps you have some answers regarding my questions and valid reasons why you have chosen to leave me and my family out of all things regarding Kathy's assets.

Kathy was my firstborn and memories of her overwhelm at times. She had a special flair for life and she spread sunshine wherever or to whomever she met. I sure miss her. All my life,

God has been my source of strength....through good and bad times. I continue to trust in His unfailing judgment! So much to deal with right now....sometimes we are dealt unbelievable crosses to bear but I am thankful I can hang on to the hand of God in all the cross roads of life. Blessing!

Now you know where I'm coming from. I put it in God's hands.... as well as all of you."

Blessings, Jean

****

This is the letter I wrote last March to Kathy's in-laws. I got one telephone call from Ron's brother, Robert, which was an hour long telling me what a great marriage they had and how wonderful Ron was. No mention of settling Kathy's assets, how much they collected or anything related to this subject. Lots of excuses why Ron didn't call an ambulance and none of them resonated with me. He went on and on for at least an hour! I'm sorry his brother died but none of his talk of excuses for Ron registered with me. This is what I got from the whole family.

I thought to myself... these people are no friends to Kathy no matter what they say. Actions matter. If they loved Kathy, as they claimed, they would have understood the hurt they put us through and would have considered a fair settlement with her family especially under the questionable circumstances. It's hard to reconcile this. My letter was quite clear. To this day, they would rather avoid me than do what's right. Kathy would not appreciate this treatment of her mother and sister.

I guess my disappointment in humanity is hard to hide. If I believed they had a truly happy marriage, I could accept a lot more. This treatment is like disrespect for my daughter. Please spare me your opinion of what a happy marriage looks like! The fact remains… he totally disregarded Kathy at the time in her life when she needed support and help the most.

My Last Letter To The Smith Family

The last letter I sent to the Smith Family trembled with a rawness that words struggled to contain. The anguish it bore emanated not only from Kathy's departure but from the harrowing circumstances surrounding it. I delved into hospital and ambulance reports, grappling with the haunting truth of negligence that led to Kathy's tragic end.

****

Subject: Kathy

To: Smith Family

"No... you don't understand. It's not that she died, but how she died that haunts me and the consideration given to me and my family to this very day. So let me try to explain.

I read through the hospital and ambulance reports and have a very hard time forgiving Ron for what happened to Kathy. Fortunately, I am filled with peace but have not come to the point of forgiveness. I don't pretend to know what the heck Ron was thinking....all I know, is that he didn't do the right thing and our family has suffered as a result of his actions. Death is the result of the lack of immediate treatment for a low blood sugar. When she passed out the first time, an ambulance should have been called.... and a call to us would have been thoughtful on his part.

Even if siblings can accept this, it's a different matter altogether for a mother. I'm sorry, but your mother should definitely have some understanding and feeling as to what I am experiencing. That I'm not supposed to express my opinions and feelings, is impossible. It was her son, Ron, Kathy's husband, and your brother who vowed to protect her through good times and bad... and unfortunately, he didn't do that.

As a result of his actions, we still suffer. It's about robbing me and her sister of being with her when she left this world...it's the haunting memory of her lying on that floor for 24 hours in pain, with no help, no 911 call and no call to us. It's her family, not being there to hold her and tell her how much we love her and us knowing how much that would have meant to her and to us. It's the nightmare of Ron's absence as a loving husband (as you claim) and us knowing that was not the case. He didn't even stay with her as she struggled for her life and then passed. This is something, I doubt, I will ever understand, or come to terms with. Words cannot possibly describe the pain and suffering our family has experienced... especially me as her mother. I'm told time heals, but under these circumstances, I can tell you, it never will for me....at least, the scar will remain.

The unforgiving thing is, he never called a priest!!! I thoroughly checked this out. I asked him to do that and he never did when he told me he would. We got the call of her critical condition a few hours before she died. Very hard to deal with.

We have been robbed of so much. Not only Ron, but you, your mother and the rest of your family continue to contribute to the pain. And, I will continue to search for answers with no apologies to anyone. We deserve answers and I'm slowly getting there. To make matters worse, you have ignored her sister and me as you collected every cent she worked for. No discussion! What's that all about? Is that something you can live with?

All this, in my opinion, tells the whole story. There was no justice for Kathy. As I think back on so many things, I now clearly see so much and my heart breaks for her as I think of all she endured. I think of her crying as the paramedics consoled her. Yes...even that is in the report. She held so much inside and her work was her escape. She was darn good at what she did. She was a complex and beautiful person, inside and outside, with an overflowing heart of love and compassion for everyone! And she would do anything for anyone if it was within her power. She had a contagious laugh and I will never hear that again.

No! You don't understand what I'm going through. I'm well aware of where you are coming from. I just lost two of the three most important loved ones of my life and I don't expect or want any words of sympathy from you. I expected justice for my daughter and fairness from the people she knew as her in-laws. Your actions during this tragic time in my life, do not meet the standard of what, I for one, and people I know, could even imagine. This would have been the time for all of you to step up to the plate and show some empathy for what happened to Kathy through sensitivity, discussion and fairness. A very big loss for all of you.

As for me, I tell it like it is. I'm sorry you are feeling resentment towards me for expressing my concerns and feelings as a mother. I'm an up front and honest person. I can't accept fantasy explanations and guessing games, especially when it comes to any one of my children. At this point, I'm searching for answers that I never got from Ron or his family. If Ron had survived, you can bet your dollar, I would be on his case for a lot that I'm finding out now. That's what you should want too. This involves the life of a human being....in this case, my daughter. I don't have her in my life...only the good memories of her along with tons of questions concerning her death and other things. Nothing is worse than that. Believe me!

I'm still waiting for a check. Didn't you say you would be taking care of this?

This email is long but you don't have to guess about where I am coming from. I lay it straight on the line. No guess work...right is right and wrong is wrong! Ron did not do the right thing and maybe someday I can forgive him but it's a struggle now. Without immediate treatment for a low blood sugar for that long, there's hardly a chance for anyone to survive. Yes. I'm having a hard time with that!

Although long...this should answer all your questions concerning us.... Kathy's family."

Jean

****

Seeking Justice For Kathy

I forwarded this detailed report to The Honorable Matt Gaetz, Florida Representative, seeking justice and closure in the wake of an agonizing loss. It's a somber commemoration of my beloved daughter, Kathleen Marie Smith, who departed this world on 09/16/2022. Her life was centered in Homestead, Florida, where she diligently served in the travel department at DelMonte.

****

"I'm a grieving mother who lost two of my three adult children in 2022. They both lived and died in Florida, just seven months apart from each other, due to diabetes. My son was 51, divorced, leaving three adult children and two grandchildren. He was diagnosed with juvenile diabetes when he was 12, had many strokes and was in a wheelchair for the last eight years of his life. I was his caregiver for most of those eight plus years. I moved him from Pennsylvania to my home in Niceville, Florida and considered it a privilege to be able to take care of him until his death.

My daughter, 61 at the time of her death, was married, had no children and lived in Homestead, Florida, in the townhouse she purchased while divorced from her husband. She later remarried him and he was on the deed of that home. She was a long-time employee at DelMonte in Coral Gables and was preparing to retire in a few months. She built up a very equitable retirement fund and financial security. Her husband was unemployed and collecting social security. He told me it was his only source of income. Her diabetes was diagnosed at the Homestead Hospital where she was taken on the evening of the 14th after passing out earlier in the week and, according to her husband, was lying on the floor for 24 hours before he finally called 911. This is also documented in the hospital report. She died a couple days later (on the 16th) due to diabetes complications. No call was made to me until a few hours before she died so we were not able to be with her. So hard! There wasn't any time to fly down to Homestead. Sadly, she died alone, except for hospital staff, who gathered around her and prayed....her husband wasn't there for some unknown reason! I will be forever thankful for every one of those hospital staff members and their kind support of her during her hospital stay and as she passed.

After living in Florida for almost 40 years, (a state I love) in September of last year, I moved to Delaware, to be near my only surviving child, my daughter and her husband. I'm 83 years old with health issues, but with the help of my daughter and son-law, I'm able to live independently. They live just a block from me...blessings for which I am truly grateful!

I have obtained the hospital records and was mortified at the over 700 pages of documented data from the moment Kathy arrived at the hospital right up to her death there. It is a stunning report. They did all they could to save her but it was an uphill battle with the diabetes diagnosis. When I became her next of kin, two months after her husband died, these hospital records were released to me upon my request. I saw pictures of her bruised 100-pound body and to this day, I can't get this out of my mind. Her husband told the admitting person she was an alcoholic and on the floor for 24 hours. She was never diagnosed as alcoholic before this.

I never saw her drink anything other than wine and only a

glass or two with me when we would be together. Having a dangerously low blood sugar, she wouldn't be drinking, even wine. I saw no tests in that report, with alcohol in her blood. His remark is hard to understand and quite defamatory. Was it to cover his negligence in getting her help? Why wouldn't he call the ambulance at the time she fell? He knew how fragile she was. The sad thing is she was at her house lying on the floor for 24 hours before she arrived, in critical condition at the hospital on September 14, and died on the 16.... we were not notified until a few hours before her death. We had no time to get to the hospital to be with her.

This was a shock! And, why wasn't this reported to law enforcement? Why didn't he call me and her sister when she fell?

I was visiting her in February after my son passed. I saw no signs of affection between the two of them. No meaningful communication. No laughter. He sat on the back porch early morning to late at night drinking beer, smoking and watching television. She had her coffee in the morning and went right to work. I felt saddened and worried about her. I asked her to come stay with me for a while and I could help her, but she said she had to finish working so she could retire at the end of the year. She would come then. She worked out of her home since covid. Never, in my wildest dreams, did I think her death would happen first!

Words do not adequately describe the painful sword piercing the heart and soul of those of us living through this kind of tragedy. The injustice only adds to the excruciating pain of losing a child; no matter the age.

In this case, his family immediately collected all her assets.

Her husband died two months after she did and then the mother-in-law inherited everything. Her family was completely ignored. Under the circumstances, this is not right. This was not what I call, a happy marriage.

My hardworking daughter was the sole provider for a secure retirement and a comfortable lifestyle after retiring. In my opinion, she provided their financial security throughout their marriage. By his admission to me, his only financial contribution was a social security check. Before he died, two months after she died, he collected everything...401K, bank account, stock account, insurance policy, house, etc. and after his death, his mother inherited every penny of it. My daughter's family received nothing. A few months before she died, I gave her 100 shares of Apple stock and asked if they would please return it to me. They kept that too!

The nightmare of my daughter's death, haunts me every day. I can't imagine her on the floor for 24 hours with no help....especially with him in the house the whole time. This kind of treatment from the one she should have trusted with her life! She left him at least twice that I know of, and divorced him another time. She was a private person but, as I look back, she never talked much about him. Now I am wondering why. I was surprised when she told me they were going to remarry. She was happy on her own, doing well and dedicated to her work.

I hope you will take the time to review this report and get back to me. Any help you can offer, will be appreciated so much. I can't understand why the hospital didn't report this neglect when she was admitted. I have tried to relate this story the best I can just highlighting points I thought were important. I hope and pray something can be done. I'm at a loss as how to proceed further. Is there any legal recourse?

Yours truly in loving memory of my daughter, Kathy, as I await your reply."

Genevieve Thomson (Jean)

****

Legal Fallout: Kathy's Story as a Call for Awareness

Florida Law:

Amendment 6 within the Florida Constitution stands as a testament to the gravity attached to criminal offenses related to disregarding the safety of another person. This particular statute highlights such actions as felonious and underscores the need for accountability in situations where someone's safety is compromised.

Furthermore, references to Amendment 7 regarding medical rights and Amendment 8, which safeguards against cruel and unusual punishment, emphasize the state's commitment to protecting individuals' rights and ensuring their well-being.

Florida Statutes, such as Section 83.515, Rule 12.740 under the Family Law Rules of Procedure, and Statutes 78.19(2), 196.131.2, and 825.1031, address various legal aspects concerning property rights, the recovery of assets, false information for financial gain, and the protection of vulnerable populations, notably the elderly or disabled adults.

The distressing incident described—an individual falling unconscious and being left unattended for an alarming 24 hours before emergency medical assistance was sought—illustrates the urgency and necessity for awareness, prevention, and swift action to protect potential victims from neglect or exploitation.

Moreover, the heart-wrenching aftermath, where the entirety of her possessions was taken by her husband, who then passed these assets to his mother without regard for her own family, highlights a troubling cycle of disregard and insensitivity.

It's evident that such vital information should be disseminated widely to shelters, hotlines, and public facilities to ensure that individuals are informed and empowered before they find themselves in vulnerable situations, unable to advocate for themselves. Far too often, victims feel trapped, hopeless, or fearful, unaware of their available options or lacking the courage to seek help.

By raising awareness and ensuring access to information about legal protections, rights, and available resources, we can offer a beacon of hope to those at risk. Empowering individuals with knowledge can serve as a lifeline, enabling them to make informed choices and seek support when faced with challenging circumstances, ultimately safeguarding themselves from exploitation or neglect.

In my pursuit of closure, I drafted a heartfelt plea to Representative Matt Gaetz, seeking assistance and a thorough review of the circumstances surrounding Kathleen's untimely demise. This email outlined my distress, the need for law enforcement involvement, and the imperative to protect my daughter's rights in the face of her tragic passing. I longed for answers, and I fervently hoped for prompt attention and assistance to address my concerns.

****

To: Representative Matt Gaetz

Re: Rights regarding law protecting deceased

"I am requesting a complete review concerning my daughter's passing, September 16, 2022. I have so many questions concerning circumstances surrounding her death and cannot find closure until I have answers. Attached, is my briefing of her tragic death and the lack of compassion for help from her then husband. Complete hospital records are available upon request.

- *Why wasn't law enforcement notified when she finally arrived at the hospital in critical condition?*

- *How does the law protect her rights when she was unable to defend or protect herself?*

Please get my request to the right department to obtain help, answers and directions for me.

I await your response and am grateful for needed help. Please help me."

Genevieve Thomson (Jean)

****

Additionally, feeling compelled to advocate for change in the wake of such unfortunate events, I penned another email to Representative Gaetz. This email proposed amendments to Florida laws, specifically addressing situations where both spouses pass away within a short period. I detailed the circumstances, suggested legal reforms, and advocated for fairness and consideration for all parties involved, drawing from my own family's painful experience. These emails became an integral part of my journey, as I sought justice and strived to ensure that others wouldn't face similar injustices.

The Honorable Matt Gaetz,

Florida Representative

"Suggest amendments to Florida laws pertaining to the death of both spouses passing within months of each other.

CIRCUMSTANCES

- *Event of spouses passing within months of each other*

- *No wills have been recorded*

- *No children involved*

- *Unanswered questions concerning death*

- *Both sides of deceased family given consideration in financial matters*

- *Questions concerning stability of marriage and intent of deceased at time of death*

LAW TO PROTECT BOTH SIDES OF DECEASED FAMILY

1. No money be disbursed for at least six months to one year in the event a surviving spouse dies within that time.

2. A thorough investigation be made to absolve and alleviate any suspicions of wrongdoing.

3. Consider both sides of family in financial settlement

4. At the resolution, then and only then, should settlement proceed perhaps by the court's direction.

My family has experienced this unfortunate situation. My story is attached. It is my hope that someone will look into this matter and take up the task to revise this law and make it fair to both sides of the family. That's all I'm asking. My family was not given any consideration or treated fairly."

Genevieve M Thomson

Mother of Kathleen Smith, deceased 09/16/2022

****

Resting in Memories

After returning from Wisconsin, where the weight of emotions engulfed me during those two intense weeks, I discovered a sense of solace slowly permeating my being. The solemn goodbyes I bid to my children eventually nudged me toward accepting a harsh reality. They were no longer here, but in a place of eternal peace, and now, my connection with them would be through spiritual communion. Until my time comes to join them, they will remain in my thoughts, prayers, and deeply missed. Their departure felt like an irrevocable loss of a significant part of myself. Yet, I must reconcile with what transpired as part of a higher plan set by God.

In our formative years, we relied on our earthly parents for guidance, and now, our faith in God's guidance becomes our anchor. Surrendering a child to the divine plan is an unfathomable emotional journey one must grapple with. But amid this turmoil, acceptance seems to be the only viable path forward. My gratitude extended immediately to my loving siblings whose compassion and support were unwavering. Despite their own health concerns, they stood by me, unable to travel as they once did. In contrast, I, too, had my share of health issues, yet I retained the ability to travel within limitations and maintain my independence.

As the eldest among my siblings, I am now part of the seven of us who remain. We endured the losses of two sisters, and my youngest brother now resides in a nursing facility. Throughout the years, our bond has only strengthened, and now, technology bridges the gaps between miles. Daily conversations over the phone and email exchanges have become our lifelines. Though not the same as physical visits, the resonance of their voices provides immeasurable comfort. I can't help but wonder if Kathy would have found solace in that same warmth if Laurie and I could have been by her side in those final days of her life. Perhaps it would have aided us too. For Kathy, I hold firm to the belief that this tragedy was held within God's control.

And so, I began to pen a letter of appreciation, an expression of gratitude and acknowledgment for the unwavering support and the bonds that have remained resolute through these trying times.

****

August 14, 2023

"Dear Family:

I'm back in Delaware after a busy and wonderful week with all of you in Wisconsin. Now I'm resting and letting all the memories absorb my thoughts. For me, the resting place for Kathy and John is finally secured and I am at peace with that. I continue to feel their presence in my life and I am grateful for that as well knowing they are together and in God's kingdom. As I like to think.... their wings were waiting for them, but our hearts were not!

I'm also blessed to be living near Laurie and Tom and grandchildren. I am totally content and reap the love and blessings every minute. What a miracle that is. Miracles all around us if only we would look around and see His Hand at work in our lives.

And a true blessing to have grown up with good Christian parents who loved us all and wanted the best for us. Their spirits remain with all of us. They did their best to prepare us for surviving in this world and to prepare for the next. Looking over that whole cemetery was an awaking time for me seeing so many I knew who have passed on...now my daughter and son join the ranks of heaven, our ultimate goal.

****

Now for the heartfelt "thank you's" from the Delaware bunch!

<u>Ralph and Kyong</u>

"I loved being with you and I thank you for all you have done for me and my family. It is so appreciated. You live next to the cemetery, so while I was at your house, I could see Kathy and John anytime from your window and walkover and talk with them. Kyong, I will never forget our heart-to-heart talks and I can never ever forget how you turned on your porch light for Kathy and John so they wouldn't be in the dark at night. You are amazing!

Thank you for everything... great food, transportation and being with Sandy and Kathy and your sweet grandchildren. Uplifting and wonderful! I have your beautiful handmade kitchen dish Pad's in my kitchen and every time I see them, I think of you. I don't spend as much time in my kitchen as you do, but it's a space that I'm in every day! Laurie was so impressed with your talent and is enjoying hers too."

****

<u>Bill and Scottie and Family</u>

"The reunion held where we grew up was spectacular as it is each year. You do a spectacular job of keeping it up. Mom and Dad are looking down with pride! Thank you for sharing it with all of us. I know it gets harder as we all get older and can't do what

we use to be able to do. All the nieces did a great job of continuing this tradition. OH MY GOSH!

I didn't realize our family grew to such unbelievable numbers. I reconnected with cousins I hadn't seen in years and even some I hadn't met. Loved all the beautiful landscaping and your choice of a band to play music we grew up on. So good to be home and be devoured in all the memories and to be surrounded by family. I pray for both of you to regain your health.

Thanks for the tour of Title town and refreshing my many great memories working for Vince Lombardi and the Green Bay Packers. Those were the days! I loved seeing my house in Green Bay too. You were an excellent tour guide. Next time I come, I'd like to see my office there. I was there the first day we moved into the new location and stadium. Lombardi would be amazed to see what he started and its Big league operation! Very impressive! Bill... quit working so hard. Scottie... take it easy and get well!"

****

<u>Tommy</u>

"You looked so good and your facility is very nice. You should be happier there. Being in a wheelchair is no fun, but remember, there are those that have it a lot worse. That seems to be life for all of us. You also have the blessing of family close by, especially Bill who does an extraordinary job of being there for you. Be happy, thankful, and grateful. I will call you soon and try to call more often. You're always in my prayers. Thank you for thinking of Kathy and John. I know they are with you too as they look down from their heavenly perch!"

****

Pat and Jerry

"I'm so sorry you are going through so much with health issues. It was great seeing you even for a short time. As always, your home and yard is breathtaking and I'm wondering how you are doing it! It's beautiful and the perfect environment for healing as all that beauty is everywhere one looks! I'm praying for your healing and good health. Now you have a great gran practically in your backyard along with having grandchildren close. Enjoy the spoiling job!"

****

Sally and Ron

"Thanks so much for spending time with me and getting me to Fond du Lac to meet Dee where my journey to Milwaukee was made possible. All the years of caregiving, didn't allow me to get to Wisconsin to be with all of you and I did miss that a lot. However, I was thrilled to meet at our favorite lunch spot and do appreciate all of you trying to put an extra few pounds on me!!! You both look great and I'm happy to see you enjoying life. Thanks for the beautiful flowers for Kathy and John. I could see them from Ralph's windows. And, for your information, your garden veggies did not go to waste. We were eating healthy!"

****

Dee and David John

"This was my final stop before leaving for Delaware where my sweet daughter and son-in-law met my plane for a 2-hour drive to our homes! I'm sure you will be resting for the next two weeks or more! There is not a better cook anywhere and it seemed like I was constantly eating all this great food! Somehow, no matter where I was, there it was! Thanks for my favorite meal

Wednesday and Friday nights.... Huge Lobster tails! Such a special treat as lobster tails around here is out of sight on price. I think I will have to encourage Tom and Laurie to take up classes on how to trap them as they spend a lot of time boating and they could be getting lobster for us while they're out there!.

DJ seems to be doing really well and looking good and that goes for Dee as well. We had a great time just being together. The first morning, I got up about 6 a.m. and sat on her lovely sun porch enjoying the morning when a beautiful cardinal flew into the trees and bushes. Shortly after that, two mourning doves flew in side by side and landed on the same bushes right in front of me.

Then the next minute, they flew off together just as they came! I was thrilled to see that and they came so close to me too! What can I say... I was totally at peace! Just great to see and be with you and DJ. My only advice would be for you to slow down a little. Thanks for all our talks, food, hugs and that delicious butterscotch sundae! Oh yes, I'm enjoying the cheese and managed to get it back with no problem. That was a heavy suitcase but I didn't have to lift it even once. I went home with tons of special memories tucked away in my heart! Thank you both!"

****

Thanks, Prayers, and Love: Blessings to All

I'm at peace with Kathy and John finally laid to rest and knowing perpetual light will shine upon them. Their spirits surround me and although I will always miss them, I know God's healing Hands will carry me through. I like to think I have many angels looking down on me and on all of us. I have lost so many loved ones. my two children, my sister Mary and her husband, Bob and Clay, my two beloved husbands, my youngest sister LaVerne, plus my Mother and Father many years ago. Also, lost a step grandson who was in his early 30's. These are all angels looking after us, and one day, there will be a great reunion at God's Kingdom!!! In the meantime, our work on earth continues and our Trust in God grows. He has strengthened my resolve, courage and strength. I would not be able to resolve these losses without my Faith! Thanks Mom and Dad. Job well done!

I had my infusion today and it went well. In two weeks, I take the second one and then I'm good for six months. My doctor set me up with temporary relief so I could make the trip to Wisconsin. I was totally comfortable pain wise. I'm doing very well today.

Laurie and Tom are taking me out boating tomorrow and they invited my wonderful neighbor couple. Should be fun. Weather is beautiful here. I made a pot of Shrimp Gumbo and had the kids come over for dinner. Allie will be leaving Saturday for her junior year at Notre Dame. It was so nice having her here for the summer. She loves Grandma's soups and loved the gumbo.

Who said I couldn't write a book!!! Please pass this on to all my wonderful nieces and nephews who arranged a super reunion. Let the next generation take the reins and hope they invite all us old folks! God bless and keep everyone in His care. Me and my family send our thanks, prayers and love!

Jeanie, Laurie, Tom, and Family

Breaking the Silence: Lessons from Personal Pain

This advice comes straight from my heart to yours...

The echoes of my daughter's absence reverberate through the hollow chambers of my heart. As a grieving mother, I grapple daily with the opaque mystery surrounding her final days. My quest for answers remains ongoing. Though justice may forever elude me, I find solace knowing her light shines on. By sharing our story, my hope is that Kathy's life continues to touch others, preventing them from walking this mournful road alone.

Kathy was always a vibrant spirit, her laugh infectious, her love of life palpable in every breath.

But privately, she shouldered heavy burdens from a young age. Scars etched deep from our family's shared trauma of abandonment and loss. She hid her vulnerabilities behind a convincing facade, loath to trouble anyone with her struggles.

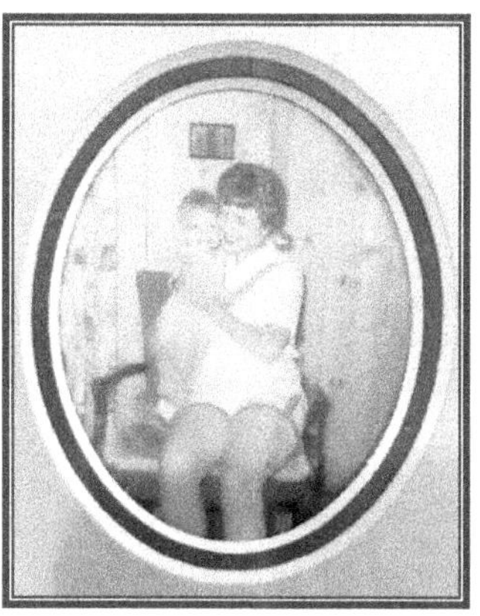

Picture of me and Kathy

I saw her quiet strength as resilience, never realizing just how much she endured silently.

If only I could retrace our steps, I'd have sheltered Kathy from the gathering storms. But she built walls to shield her crumbling interior. My warnings went unheeded, my concern written off as maternal fussing. She insisted all marriages have ups and downs. But the red flags flew high, even as I doubted my misgivings.

In retrospect, the signs glare obvious. The light in Kathy's eyes dimmed over time. Laughter came less easily as her spontaneous spirit grew subdued. She withdrew further after each separation, reluctant to unburden her heart. I opened my door, promised unwavering support, but she remained resolute - this was her cross to bear.

How many mothers will recognize their daughter's quiet despair in Kathy's story? Your intuition is seldom wrong. Trust those instincts, even when your child rejects interference. Abuse festers in silence. The vice of isolation and control tightens its grip by imperceptible degrees. She needed me to override her protests. If only I had been more adamant in prying open that gilded cage.

But the melancholy wisdom of hindsight rings hollow. I cannot rewrite our history, cannot undo her suffering or erase her pain. What is done cannot be undone. The road of second guesses leads nowhere but regret. Forgiveness remains the only path to peace.

So, I move forward carrying these difficult lessons, hoping they can steer others from this anguished terrain. My daughter's gentle spirit will endure as her legacy. By offering this story, her life continues rippling outwards, touching more souls than she ever knew.

To all parents: our job never ends, no matter how old our children grow. Their headaches become heartaches, but our love remains their strongest medicine. Keep communication open, even when paths diverge. Visit often, listen without judgement. See beyond their platitudes and assurances. If possible, gently guide them home when you sense they've lost their way.

<u>Red Flags:</u> Drastic shifts in personality should raise concerns. Withdrawal from loved ones allows problems to fester unseen. Remain vigilant for signs of volatility or control in your child's partner. I ignored these red flags to my eternal regret. Intervene before patterns cement. Make it clear your door remains open, no matter what.

If your child is enduring domestic troubles, separation may be healthiest. Some unions should not persist. Walking away requires courage, but serenity awaits those who choose self-love. Encourage therapy for both parties to illuminate root causes. Abuse often stems from generational trauma. Darkness cannot drive out darkness - only light can do that. With patient work, reconciliation may even follow. But the safety of your child must come first.

<u>Advise Legal Counsel:</u> Should grievous loss leave you seeking answers, act quickly to protect your rights. Engage a trusted attorney experienced in such matters. Their counsel overrides well-meaning but ill-informed opinions of family and friends. Time is of the essence - flickers of memory fade, evidence disappears. Allow no room for doubt or guilt to make you hesitate. Fight for the truth your child deserves.

In retrospect, I waited far too long, lulled into inaction by shock and despair. Seemingly insurmountable obstacles loomed between me and the opaque mysteries surrounding Kathy's end. So I retreated into my grief, paralyzed by uncertainty and fear. Don't follow my example - move forward with relentless purpose. The truth may prove elusive, but the journey holds value. You'll emerge wiser, with hard-won conviction that our temporal forms cannot contain our eternal spirits.

No matter where this grief-stricken path leads you, have faith your loved one walks beside you still. Their essence lives on, whispers on the breeze, in sunlight through the leaves, in quiet moments of remembrance. Each soul on earth has chapters left unwritten. But our Creator pens the final act. We need only play our imperfect part as best we can, then trust the rest to His divine plan.

Though Kathy's role in my story concluded too soon, the gifts of her life linger. Her infectious laughter echoes, her unwavering love sustains me. She was a caretaker, a loyal confidante, quick to lift others when life weighed heavy. She'd want her struggles to shed light, helping another avoid her fate. So I honor her best by spreading compassion, by embracing each moment as the gift it is.

My daughter leaves a legacy of resilience, of courage culled from adversity, of squeezing joy from every ordinary day. I strive now to view the world through her eyes - to laugh long and loud, savor small delights, reach out in empathy, and above all, refuse to take one breath for granted.

Kathy will forever be the brilliant light guiding me home. And through me, she now guides you. May her story plant seeds of change, of hope. May her memory be a blessing, awakening courage and vision in all who need it. Our children never truly leave us. They remain within our hearts, and in the hearts of every person their lives have touched.

Enduring Echoes

Returning to Delaware, I reflect on the intense weeks in Wisconsin and acknowledge a sense of solace gradually permeating my being. Bidding solemn goodbyes to my children have nudged me toward accepting a harsh reality – they are no longer here, but in a place of eternal peace. Until my time comes to join them, our connection remains through spiritual communion. The memories of Kathy overwhelm me at times; she had a special flair for life, spreading sunshine wherever she went.

I always think of Kathy and John when I see this beautiful painting!

Little did I know or even think there was any chance for me to ever find peace and happiness again after such horrendous losses. I am discovering, for those who believe and trust in God, the journey of life continues on a whole new highway. Gradually, one wakes up to days filled with hope again and the comforting thought of feeling safe and secure in God's hands. I will never leave you alone becomes a true feeling of trust.

Only nowadays, I realize how strong my foundation of faith has always been to survive the storms in my life. I realize there was no way I could have gone through all of this without a complete dependence on a power greater than mine. This realization fills me with peace and love beyond expectation. In spite of the heartbreaks, I was gifted beyond words and have no doubt, my help was coming from divine intervention. Someone above, loved me and my family and was there to help.

Laurie flew down to Florida on September 4, 2022, and with friends, put together the final touches for our drive to Delaware. That day was special for me as it was Bob's birthdate, so naturally I was expecting him to be with us in spirit. He was too!

Laurie and I had great alone time. We stopped to see grandchildren along the way. Before I knew it, we were at my new home. I was about to find a whole new life here, and at that point, I had no idea how absolutely necessary it was and what a Godsend to end up here... safe, sound and miraculously!

This would definitely be a new beginning for me. Being close to family, would be exactly what I needed to regain strength and healing and to have a purpose to wake up in the morning. This was a chance for me to gain a new lease on life. Get it back on track.

I soon discovered that I needed plenty of rest and relaxation, not to mention lots of alone time to allow my brain and body to relax and evaluate my options... to look reality straight in the eye and regain my positive manner. I needed God given peace to function. I had no idea what it would take to be happy again in a world turned upside down but I knew it was up to me. I had never entertained a negative attitude so I drastically needed an attitude adjustment. There was a time to mourn but I couldn't stay stuck there. I had to allow rays of sunshine to illuminate days ahead.

Hearing about Kathy's death, almost finished my desire to even try. I wanted to go to bed, cover my head with the blanket and wake up in a world that would magically take away all these horrific realities that I was having a hard time coping with.

After Kathy's funeral, I made a choice to trust in God's judgment for the road ahead. However, He would have to show me the way. I had her and her brother for many years and I was thankful for that. Kathy had no children but John had three plus two grandsons and they were part of him. They were an extension of my son, and although his children were now adults, they would always be part of me as well. Kathy's situation was so much different. I had no closure due to the circumstances of her death. Eventually, I know justice will prevail for her too. I truly believe that.

Better yet, I had one beautiful, amazing daughter to cherish and love and now I was living a block from her and her loving husband. How wonderful was that! Laurie and Tom are an amazing couple and parents. My beautiful and amazing daughter, has energy for life and unlimited talent to match her many endeavors. She married a man who supported her efforts in whatever she tackled. They are each other's best friend. Most importantly, he is a wonderful husband and father. I loved seeing that.

They are both retired now after raising and educating five beautiful children; some married with families of their own. The youngest started her 3rd year at Notre Dame. I look forward to her college breaks to spend time with her. She is a perfect example of so many young people today who do have goals for their futures. Goals that are good and constructive. I look forward to many more of our wonderful talks.

I'm able to participate in family activities. Blessings beyond what I could have imagined. Now that all my grandchildren are adults, I'm watching my great grandchildren grow up. The empty spaces in my heart, are being filled to overflowing with love all around me.

Life goes on and it's not leaving me behind!

Even if I didn't know what was best for me, God did. I needed to put my trust in His powerful care. Regardless of my insurmountable losses, I recognized all the unbelievable blessings now and throughout my lifetime.

The letter, penned on August 14, 2023, serves as an

expression of gratitude to family members who provided unwavering support during those trying times.

As I share snippets of my recent life, from family reunions to medical updates, I aim to convey a sense of resilience rooted in faith. The challenges of health issues, distance, and loss have strengthened the bond among my siblings, bridged by technology. In the face of adversity, we find comfort in daily conversations, nurturing the connections that transcend physical presence. I also touch upon the moments of solace and serenity, finding peace in the embrace of nature and the support of loved ones.

In closing, I express my trust in God's unfailing judgment and acknowledge the crosses we bear. Despite the unbelievable challenges, I find solace in holding onto God's hand at the crossroads of life. The letter is a testament to my journey, acknowledging the pain, the losses, and the enduring faith that sustains me.

I didn't write this book for money. In fact, it never even entered my mind. My purpose was to help others navigate through my experiences. To have hope and courage when life throws those curve balls and catches us off guard. Tears are healing and cleansing for the soul. I've definitely had my share. I was drowning in tears, and only God's help, turned the darkness into light.

But those tears can also build strength, hope and a firm determination to make the best of God's gifts. We all have a purpose in this life. I know that doing the right thing produces rewards that will not only help us in this world, but in God's court, will help us enter into the next when our work on earth is done. That's what I'm hoping for all who read my story.

Walk with God. He's our salvation in all things that are good!

I still have three beautiful children. My gifts from God... one on earth and two in heaven! Kathy and John live in my heart as well. My life is richly blessed!